Praise for Michael Hyatt and His Previous Books

Free to Focus

"Michael Hyatt is one of _____ ders rely on smart systems to _____ vell as at home, and *Free to _____* ur system that every smart leader cr_____

John C. Maxwell, author, speaker, and leadership expert

"Michael Hyatt has written the guide to creating freedom and money without burning ourselves out in the process. . . . You will be able to work in a space where nothing is urgent, deadlines are met, and the workday truly ends at the office."

Brooke Castillo, founder, The Life Coach School

"Busyness is meaningless. What matters is consistently executing the work that actually matters. This book shows you how."

Cal Newport, *New York Times* bestselling author, *Deep Work* and *Digital Minimalism*

"Michael Hyatt's practical approach to productivity isn't just another tactical guide filled with good ideas—it's a comprehensive strategy for overhauling your life. It's not just about getting more done, but getting the right things done—and that starts by knowing where you want to go."

Ruth Soukup, *New York Times* bestselling author, *Do It Scared*

"A fantastic guide—filled with actionable advice and tools— to maximize your energy, your focus, and your results."

Kevin Kruse, *New York Times* bestselling author, *15 Secrets Successful People Know about Time Management*

"A practical, flexible framework for centering your life around what matters most, and unleashing your best work every day."

Todd Henry, author, *The Accidental Creative*

"The steps in *Free to Focus* are clear, the strategies are actionable, and the lessons are timeless. Like me, you may find yourself wanting to reread this powerful book again and again."

Jeff Sanders, speaker and author, *The 5 AM Miracle*

"Michael Hyatt shines the light on the secrets of the most productive people."

Skip Prichard, CEO, OCLC, Inc.; *Wall Street Journal* bestselling author, *The Book of Mistakes*

"I'm proud to claim Michael as my go-to authority. His brave leadership teaches practical productivity principles that have yielded extraordinary results for myself and the others who he walks alongside in the trenches of life."

Erik Fisher, podcast host, *Beyond the To-Do List*

"Michael's no-nonsense, all-helpful advice can help anyone prioritize their life to do more of what's important to them."

Chris Guillebeau, author, *Side Hustle* and *The $100 Startup*

"Michael Hyatt has proven the system where it counts—in the field, with real entrepreneurs and real corporate leaders.

Steven Robbins, creator, Get-it-Done Groups; podcast host, *Get-It-Done Guy's Quick and Dirty Tips to Work Less and Do More*

"Great stories are thought through before they're written. Great lives are the same. Mike gives us a framework to plan our lives in such a way we won't have to experience regret."

Donald Miller, *New York Times* bestselling author; founder and CEO, StoryBrand

Your Best Year Ever

"Throughout your life, you'll meet three types of leaders. The first inspires ambition, without results. The second improves results, but ignores the spirit. . . . Michael Hyatt proves he is the rare third type of leader—one who both raises our performance and lifts our soul."

Sally Hogshead, *New York Times* bestselling author;
creator, How to Fascinate®

"A simple program, backed by the best modern research, to reach your dreams!"

Tony Robbins, #1 *New York Times* bestselling author,
Unshakeable

"Michael Hyatt has a knack for making the complex simple. Even better, he makes it useful."

Dan Sullivan, president, The Strategic Coach Inc.

"Michael Hyatt has created a fun, fast way to find your dreams and then turn them into reality."

Seth Godin, author, *Linchpin*

"For more than a decade, I've known Michael as a successful leader and entrepreneur. Now . . . he shares the simple, proven system he uses to achieve his most important goals. This book can help you achieve even more than you thought possible."

Andy Stanley, senior pastor, North Point
Community Church; author, *Visioneering*

"The best resource on goal setting I've read."

Jon Gordon, *New York Times* bestselling author,
The Energy Bus

"Must-read for business people, athletes, parents, students, teachers, public officials, volunteers, or anyone else who wants to have greater influence and impact and a more effective personal and professional life."

Tim Tassopoulos, president and COO, Chick-fil-A, Inc.

"There are many people who talk about goals, but listen to Michael. He grounds this advice in sound research. A great guide."

Dr. Henry Cloud, psychologist; *New York Times* bestselling author

"Not only am I having our whole team at FranklinCovey read *Your Best Year Ever*, I am having my three college-age children read it as well. Michael gives us a profound road map for both hope and achievement!"

Chris McChesney, coauthor, *The 4 Disciplines of Execution*

"Say goodbye to #goalfailure once you learn Michael Hyatt's *Best Year Ever* goal-setting system. His teaching is rooted in the best science available, and the proof is in the gritty, real-life stories of average people who have achieved extraordinary results."

Amy Porterfield, host, *The Online Marketing Made Easy* podcast

"Following this process has led to my most successful and fulfilling year ever."

Pat Flynn, author, *Will It Fly?*; host, *Smart Passive Income* podcast

"Hands down, the best goal-setting program I have ever seen."

Jeff Goins, bestselling author, *The Art of Work* and *Real Artists Don't Starve*

"Equal parts Albert Einstein, Mark Twain, and Jack Welch."

Andy Andrews, *New York Times* bestselling author, *The Traveler's Gift* and *The Noticer*

"Helps you build a very solid framework for setting better goals and then achieving them. You'll benefit from his research and the great ideas he's synthesized here for your success."

Chris Brogan, *New York Times* bestselling author,
It's Not About the Tights

Living Forward (coauthored with Daniel Harkavy)

"Full of reminders and revelation that will open up your mind and organize your time."

Dave Ramsey, *New York Times* bestselling author,
The Total Money Makeover

"Here is an extremely practical and undeniably necessary guide for any adult who has drifted from how they thought life should be lived. I have benefited from this approach in my own life, but I need to be reminded again and again and again."

Patrick Lencioni, president, the Table Group;
author, *The Five Dysfunctions of a Team*
and *The Advantage*

"A fully customizable blueprint to achieve the design and execution of the life you want to live."

Chalene Johnson, *New York Times* bestselling author;
CEO, Team Johnson

"An intelligent and articulate manual for recognizing the more elevated (and subtle) aspects of our commitments and expressions, and appropriately engaging with them. Applying even a portion of its simple and practical recommendations will improve anyone's condition in life. Bravo!"

David Allen, *New York Times* bestselling author,
Getting Things Done

"*Living Forward* gives readers a simple and proven process for identifying what matters most and creating a life with less of the rest."

Fawn Weaver, *New York Times* bestselling author, *The Argument-Free Marriage*; founder, The Happy Wives Club

"The power of *Living Forward* lies in the elegant simplicity of the book—it is a short book with a long and lasting impact. Using this book, you can create your own Life Plan in a single day, and quite literally change the course of your life."

Ray Edwards, host, *The Ray Edwards Show*; founder, Ray Edwards International

"Michael Hyatt and Daniel Harkavy have much to teach us. In a world of random, often directionless lives, their lives stand out as examples of careers well chosen, time well used, and passion deeply heeded."

Max Lucado, *New York Times* bestselling author, *Fearless* and *Outlive Your Life*

"A brilliant and motivating resource."

Lysa Terkeurst, *New York Times* bestselling author; president, Proverbs 31 Ministries

"You can either intentionally pursue the essential or you can unintentionally drift into the nonessential. This book brilliantly teaches how to do the former while avoiding the latter. Read it and live it—you will love it."

Greg McKeown, *New York Times* bestselling author, *Essentialism*

THE
VIS ON
DR VEN
LEADER

THE VIS|ON DR|VEN LEADER

10 QUESTIONS TO FOCUS YOUR EFFORTS, ENERGIZE YOUR TEAM, AND SCALE YOUR BUSINESS

MICHAEL HYATT

BakerBooks

a division of Baker Publishing Group
Grand Rapids, Michigan

Published by Baker Books
a division of Baker Publishing Group
PO Box 6287, Grand Rapids, MI 49516-6287
www.bakerbooks.com

Printed in the United States of America

Library of Congress Cataloging-in-Publication Data
Names: Hyatt, Michael S., author.
Title: The vision-driven leader : 10 questions to focus your efforts, energize your team, and scale your business / Michael Hyatt.
Description: Grand Rapids : Baker Books, a division of Baker Publishing Group, 2020.
Identifiers: LCCN 2019036029 | ISBN 9780801075278 (cloth)
Subjects: LCSH: Employees—Coaching of. | Leadership.
Classification: LCC HF5549.5.C53 H93 2020 | DDC 658.4/092—dc23
LC record available at https://lccn.loc.gov/2019036029

ISBN 978-0-8010-9499-6 (ITPE)

The author is represented by Alive Literary Agency, 7680 Goddard Street, Suite 200, Colorado Springs, CO 80920, www.alive literary.com

20 21 22 23 24 25 26   7 6 5 4 3 2

Contents

PART 1

VISION DRIVES EVERYTHING

The ability to envision possibilities for the future and share that vision with others distinguishes leaders from nonleaders.

HERMINIA IBARRA

What defines a good leader? Enabling other people to step into the unseen.

BEAU LOTTO

A leader has the vision and conviction that a dream can be achieved. He inspires the power and energy to get it done.

RALPH LAUREN

Are You a Leader or a Manager?

The Cost of Confusion

> Those who look only to the past or present are certain to miss the future.
>
> JOHN F. KENNEDY[1]

I grew up at the dawn of the space age. My school years were full of Tom Swift books and dreams of interplanetary travel. I geeked out on science and technology, saw every movie I could, read every comic book I could, and spent countless hours drawing spaceships of my own, meticulously adding every necessary detail for the galactic voyages I hoped to make. I wanted to be an astronaut. But it wasn't just sci-fi that lit my rockets. America was then in the midst of a very real space race.

The Soviet Union started things off by launching the world's first satellite, Sputnik 1, in October 1957. I was a little more than two years old at the time. Then in April

1961, when I was almost six, Soviet cosmonaut Yuri Gagarin became the first human to orbit Earth. It was a tremendous achievement, but we Americans were in no mood to celebrate. During the height of the Cold War, tensions were stratospheric. At best, Soviet success in space spelled a loss of American prestige. At worst, it posed an existential threat. American school students my age and older were required to participate in "duck and cover" drills under their desks in case of a nuclear attack. Backyard bomb shelters were all the rage. As the arms race intensified, everyone was asking, What if the Russians could weaponize space? Americans needed to respond. But how?

Though the Soviets had the upper hand, US president John F. Kennedy viewed space as a critical Cold War battleground. His predecessor disagreed. President Dwight Eisenhower only begrudgingly established NASA and funded the Mercury program. Eisenhower's reluctance was understandable but resulted in the Soviets going farther, faster than the US, and as one writer put it, "added to the national inferiority complex" Americans felt.[2]

Kennedy was convinced America could not afford to cede more ground to the Soviet Union. So six weeks after Gagarin's flight, he stood before a joint session of Congress and made the biggest sales pitch of his presidency. "Now it is time . . . for this nation to take a clearly leading role in space achievement, which in many ways may hold the key to our future on earth," he said before outlining his specific goal:

> I believe that this nation should commit itself to . . . landing
> a man on the moon and returning him safely to the earth. No
> single space project in this period will be more impressive to

mankind, or more important for the long-range exploration of space; and none will be so difficult or expensive to accomplish. . . . It will not be one man going to the moon—if we make this judgment affirmatively, it will be an entire nation. For all of us must work to put him there.[3]

Many at the time considered Kennedy's vision delusional. They doubted we could land on the moon with the available technology and know-how—let alone bring an astronaut back alive. Eisenhower called Kennedy's announcement "hysterical," and viewed his "spectacular dash to the moon" as "nuts" and a "stunt."[4] NASA's first administrator, T. Keith Glennan, was equally unsupportive. He called the president's plan "a very bad move."[5]

Public disbelief and criticism remained as the project progressed. From June 1961 through July 1967, pollsters asked the public: "Would you favor or oppose US government spending to send astronauts to the Moon?" Less than half of the public was in favor, excluding one month during my tenth year when the majority opinion briefly swung toward the moon shot.[6]

Thankfully, Kennedy knew what every vision-driven leader knows: if the vision is compelling enough, people will apply their best thinking and efforts to figure it out, regardless of the obstacles and opposition. Kennedy called upon "every scientist, every engineer, every serviceman, every technician, contractor, and civil servant [to give] his personal pledge that this nation will move forward, with the full speed of freedom, in the exciting adventure of space."[7] Despite the naysayers, people stepped up to transform the president's vision to reality.

The effort faced incredible challenges and catastrophic setbacks, and though Kennedy was not alive to celebrate

If the vision is compelling enough, people will apply their best thinking and efforts to figure it out, regardless of the obstacles and opposition.

the achievement, on July 20, 1969, Neil Armstrong emerged from Apollo 11 and became the first man to set foot on the moon. He even did it ahead of schedule. I had turned fourteen the month before, and I don't recall ever having been more elated, more amazed, than I was at that moment. Armstrong safely splashed down in the Pacific on July 24, but despite my elation, the hard truth is it took a lot longer for the real lesson of the moon shot to land for me. Like countless kids my age, I eventually traded my desire to become an astronaut for the dream of starting a business. Armstrong's moonwalk testified to what a leader's vision can accomplish. But even though that lesson unfolded before my adolescent eyes, it took the catastrophic failure of my first business years later to teach me what Kennedy showed the entire world.

I'll tell you that story in the coming pages, along with what I did to rebound, but first let me just say this. In the decades following that failure, I've come back to successfully lead teams and companies. I've been an executive, and I've coached executives. And through all those experiences, I've discovered something else: I'm far from the only leader who has struggled with vision.

The Vision Thing

Whenever I reflect on the success of Kennedy's moon shot, I can't help but compare it with the story of another American president.

George H. W. Bush had a reputation for lacking vision. In 1987, he was running for office and knew he needed a way to connect with voters. He asked a colleague to identify some issues that would resonate. Not so fast, said the friend.

According to *Time*, instead of providing a litany of winning issues, he "suggested that Bush go alone to Camp David for a few days to figure out where he wanted to take the country." "Oh," responded Bush, unimpressed by the idea, "the vision thing."[8] Bush possessed many positive qualities but saw taking time to craft a vision as pointless, uninteresting, or too difficult. It wasn't his thing. And that cost him. Rightly or wrongly, critics saw Bush as a yes-man with little presence or power of his own. "What does Bush really stand for?" asked reporter Margaret Garrard Warner in a provocative cover story for *Newsweek* entitled "Bush Battles the 'Wimp Factor.'" He was, she said, "by and large a politician without a political identity."[9]

Thanks in part to hard campaigning and a soft opponent, Bush managed to win the election, but observers noted that the lack of "the vision thing" plagued his presidency. Kennedy had the luxury of an intolerable situation; Russia's aggressive stance forced a creative response. But when faced with his own challenges—including an economic recession and changing global landscape—Bush failed to chart a compelling course for the country.

Some believed he lacked the strength or courage to lead. They saw him as a manager, not a leader, and that perception ultimately undermined his 1992 reelection bid.[10] Unable to cast a vision of a profitable economy or America's role in a post–Cold War world, Bush failed to get the votes.

Vision is the essential ingredient for successful leadership. There's no substitute. Without it, influence fades along with the crowds. This is especially true in business. Unless you, as a leader, have a clear picture of the destination where you want your company to be in three to five years, you've got nothing that will inspire people to follow you. "Leaders create things that didn't exist before," Seth Godin says. "They do this by giving the tribe a vision of something that could happen, but hasn't (yet)."[11]

This is the primary difference between leaders and managers. When asked by *Harvard Business Review*, "What makes a good manager?" GE's legendary chairman and CEO Jack Welch responded with a crucial clarification. "I prefer the term 'business leader,'" he said. "Good business leaders create a vision, articulate the vision, passionately own the vision, and relentlessly drive it to completion."[12]

Vision is the essential ingredient for successful leadership.

Voters expected Bush to act like a leader; instead, he behaved like a manager. Both roles are important, but they are fundamentally different and require different dispositions and skill sets. Leaders create vision, while managers execute vision. Leaders inspire and motivate, while managers maintain and administer. Leaders take risks, while managers control risks. Leaders stay focused on the horizon, while managers have their eye on short-term goals and objectives. "The manager is the classic good soldier," as pioneering leadership-studies author Warren Bennis said; whereas, "the leader is his or her own person."[13]

There are significant consequences for getting these backward. Research conducted by the Corporate Executive Board noted an uptick in dysfunctional decision-making within organizations among managers. "Today's organizations require an average of 5.4 managers reaching consensus to make a decision," they found, elaborating,

> The 5.4 typically hail from different functional areas within the company and often have conflicting goals, motivations,

and perspectives. . . . In that type of environment, the result is not bad decision-making—it's no decision-making whatsoever, keeping the status quo. The second alternative chosen by the 5.4 is to proceed with the least risky, lowest-cost path forward. Quality and customer impact take a backseat to price.[14]

You'll never get to the moon like that. "Leadership," as Sheryl Sandberg, Facebook's celebrated chief operating officer, says, "is the art of accomplishing more than the science of management teaches you is possible." And that, she says, requires a vision "that can take you from where you are to the more-than-foreseeable future."[15]

So how do I define this essential ingredient?

THE LEADER-MANAGER DIFFERENTIAL

Leaders	Managers
Create and cast vision	Receive and execute vision
Inspire and motivate	Maintain and administer
Weigh and take risks	Control and minimize risks
Focus on the long term	Focus on the short term

The Essential Ingredient

Vision, as I see it, is a clear, inspiring, practical, and attractive picture of your organization's future. It doesn't have to be ten or twenty years down the road, though that might be helpful.[16] I'm talking about an imagined future—usually just three to five years out—superior to the present, which motivates you, which guides day-to-day strategy and decision-making, and around which your team can rally.

Without this, you're effectively voting for the status quo. Your organization doesn't need a leader unless they want to

VISION   **NO VISION**

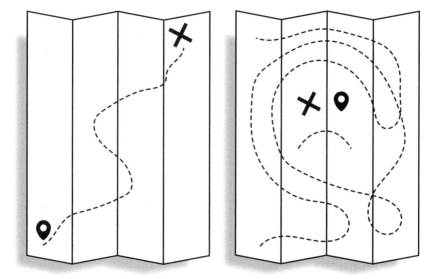

Vision is the difference between knowing where you're going and traveling in circles.

change. It doesn't take a leader to maintain the status quo. A competent manager will do just fine. If, however, you find the status quo unacceptable and want to focus your efforts, energize your team, and scale your business, you must be a vision-driven leader.

That is what this book is all about. By formulating a compelling vision of the future, as Kennedy did, leaders can achieve what was previously considered impossible. They can develop meaningful strategies, attract A-plus talent, and take their organizations to new and exciting places. But for many leaders, it's not as easy or straightforward as it sounds. You might be one of them, and I really can't blame you.

In his book *What You Don't Know About Leadership but Probably Should,* Baylor professor Jeffrey Kottler defines vision as the "initial task" of leaders.[17] It's the first thing, the top priority.

But in my experience as the chairman and chief executive officer of Thomas Nelson Publishers, one of the world's largest English-language publishers before its 2011 acquisition by HarperCollins, and now as the CEO of my own leadership-coaching company, I find many leaders are more like Bush than Kennedy.

Through no fault of their own, they're often dismissive of, confused about, and ill-equipped to create compelling visions for their organizations. Why? Let's roll through these three problems as we move toward the solution.

1. Leaders downplay the need. Bush was impatient with developing his vision, and I see that same tendency among some of the business owners and executives I've coached over the years. I even worked for a CEO like that. He wouldn't make time for vision. He didn't think it was his strength or even his responsibility.

Instead, he appointed a committee, put me in charge of it, and said, "You guys do the vision thing. Come up with a vision for where we're going, and then let me know what you've decided." Instead of sending us off on our own, he could have—should have—joined us at the table. If he had, his executives could have asked him the kind of probing questions necessary to arrive at a vision he could endorse, the sorts of questions upon which this book is based. More on that in a moment.

My old boss is not alone. Contemporary leadership suffers from a vision deficit. According to one study of 466 companies, respondents identified the following as one of the top-felt corporate deficiencies: "Leaders who can create a compelling vision and engage others around it." What's more, that "need was both a top priority *and* also perceived as the most lacking competency in next-generation leaders."[18] Similarly, in her work analyzing hundreds of 360-degree managerial assessments, INSEAD professor Herminia Ibarra says vision is one leadership skill in which most subjects come up short.[19] A large number of leaders view vision as secondary. That's because there's an action bias inherent to leadership. Execution, after all, is right there in the word—*executive*. These leaders limit their job to effective execution of their current objectives. That's necessary, but insufficient. Execution is just part of the picture. Without a destination and the people to follow you there, you might be busy, but you're not busy leading your company.

Part of this can be explained because leaders haven't been coached on the benefits and payoff that being vision-driven brings to their organization. Author Suzanna Bates observes, "Confidence and Vision paired together breed a distinct kind of optimism in an organization. They ignite a sense that it's okay to take a risk, try something new, and push ahead. When confident leaders express a frame-changing vision, they inspire those around them to take bold action."[20]

One of the things we have to do as leaders is to create or point to a larger purpose and story. Our teams want something that requires their best effort, that requires innovation in their thinking, that inspires their imagination. And it's up to us to ask ourselves, Does what we're trying to do as an organization create that kind of inspiration? Is it something that's challenging, or just business as usual?

2. Leaders are confused about vision. One reason there's such an absence of vision-driven leadership these days stems from a misunderstanding about vision. As you'll see in Question 3, vision is not the same as mission. Nor is it the same as strategy, something we'll cover in Question 6.

Vision is an act of seeing what the future could be, and then articulating that potential in an inspiring, clear, practical, and attractive way—what I call a Vision Script—which the leader's teams can then follow into the future. That's what vision-driven leaders like George Eastman did with photography, Henry Ford did with the automobile, and Steve Jobs did with personal computing. They instinctively knew that people are looking for something to believe in, an outcome to embrace, a winning aspiration.

Leaders also make the mistake of thinking of vision as a static quality or a quirk of personality; either you have a powerful vision, like Kennedy, or you don't, like Bush. But a compelling vision of the future is really something anyone can develop if they know how. And it's something vital to develop, because our ultimate success and failure is on the line. You'll be glad to know the questions in this book will point the way.

When we have a compelling, unifying view of the future, and when we communicate it to the team with passion and purpose, it can motivate people to accomplish astonishing things. Those who lack vision—or, more to the point, won't give it the proper attention—are unready for the challenge of leadership.

I've witnessed this transformative power of vision while coaching thousands of business leaders to win at work and succeed at life. But a vision will work only if you're willing to do the necessary work to craft one. Kennedy did the heavy lifting of getting clear on what he wanted, and America responded by doing the impossible. I wonder if Bush ever regretted skipping that trip to Camp David.

3. Leaders don't feel equipped. One of the reasons leaders downplay vision or don't see the need for it is self-protection. They feel ill-equipped to create and cast a compelling picture of the future. Like my old boss, the prospect leaves them feeling uncomfortable or worse.

No one enjoys doing something that feels foreign to their skill set, but this challenge is especially tough for leaders. Why? Because we assume they're supposed to have all the answers. They're supposed to be the most competent, the most in command. When leaders come up short on vision, it's like admitting a weakness or a shortcoming. It seems easier to downplay "the vision thing" and jump to tasks at which they excel: strategy, execution, team building, whatever.

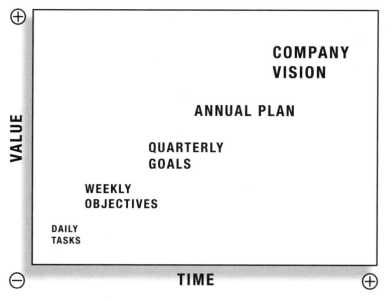

If you, as a leader, compare the relative time horizons, daily and weekly tasks can feel more important than your vision—*it's so far out there!* But if you look at the relative value, working on your vision stands out as the most important task on a leader's list. In Question 6, I'll show how these activities work together.

At Michael Hyatt & Co., we conduct leadership-coaching intensives through our BusinessAccelerator program. I often hear from men and women who started a business or found themselves promoted into positions of responsibility and now feel the pressure to level up. They know that involves vision, but they feel unprepared. Some feel as if they're imposters—as if it's only a matter of time before they're found out and lose it all.

I've been there. I get it. And there's a simple reason for the prevalence of this feeling. They've never had the coaching to create a compelling picture of the future, something desirable, exciting, and challenging to motivate their teams. If that's you, I've got good news. *The Vision Driven Leader* will show you how to craft a compelling vision and use it to guide your company forward with intention and energy.

Your Plan for Vision-Driven Success

You picked up this book because you're either a leader, or you aspire to be one. *The Vision Driven Leader* is organized around a series of ten questions to help you create and cast your vision; make it clear, inspiring, and practical; sell it to your team; and weather the challenges ahead.

Together, the questions work like a diagnostic tool to help you focus on what matters and get the answers you need to channel your efforts, energize your team, and grow your business bigger than you ever thought possible. These questions also function like the interlocking parts of a proven vision-crafting system; address them honestly and you'll leave with a powerful vision you can deploy in your organization. Let me briefly walk you through each before we explore them in depth in the pages ahead.

Question 1: Are you a leader or a manager? As you already know from reading this far, both roles are valuable and necessary for any business to succeed. But, as you also know, they're very different roles. Leaders and managers view the world and approach their work through different lenses. By confusing these roles, companies drift, struggle, and eventually fail.

Question 2: What difference does vision make? Next, we'll discover the six pitfalls of vision-deficit leaders. Don't worry if some hit close to home. They sure did for me, especially early in my career. In this question, I'll reveal how I learned the value of vision in one of the hardest ways possible—my own colossal business failure. Absent future focus, leaders frustrate their teams and waste precious resources, time, and talent; we'll look at one company, for instance, that burned through $900 million in funding before folding because they had no clear vision of the future.

Question 3: What do you want? Here we'll differentiate mission and vision, and I'll share how vision helped me salvage a dying division when I unexpectedly found myself as the head of the department. We'll cover three tips for composing a powerful Vision Script around four interrelated futures: the future of your team, the future of your products, the future of your sales and marketing efforts, and the future of the impact that your company can have on the world.

Question 4: Is it clear? Now that you've identified what you want, the next step is to ensure what's in your head is clear so you can effectively communicate it. Here I'll guide you through the three land mines to avoid when addressing your team: namely, intuitive, confusing, and flat-out foggy communication. Clarity comes when your vision is concrete rather than abstract and your communication is explicit rather than implicit. I'll share a simple model, the Vision Grid, to help visualize what true clarity involves.

Question 5: Does it inspire? If your Vision Script doesn't fire your rockets, you won't be able to help your team reach liftoff—and some might not even join you on the launchpad. That's why, after clarity, it's essential your vision be inspiring to you and others. You'll learn the value of focusing on what isn't rather than on what is. You'll see the benefit of an exponential vision over an incremental vision. We'll discuss the difference between a vision that's risky and one that's just plain stupid. And we'll also see why your Vision Script should focus on *what* you envision, not *how* you're going to get it done.

Question 6: Is it practical? A compelling vision does more than imagine a desired future. It's practical enough to guide your actions in the present, particularly in two key areas: your plan and your people. Without it, you'll hire poorly, work aimlessly, and fill the weeks and months with meaningless activity instead of the kind of focused effort it takes to reach your destination.

Question 7: Can you sell it? The surest test of your Vision Script is whether you can sell it to your team. When you first craft your vision, it's wet cement. You need to involve key stakeholders before it's finalized and before you roll it out companywide. This requires a bit of a dance. Here I'll help you sell it up the chain, down the chain, across the organization, and even outside of the company. Without that, you won't have your intended impact.

Question 8: How should you face resistance? Every vision encounters resistance. It's inherent to the act of taking what isn't and bringing it into being. But, as a colleague of mine used to say, "If it was easy, they wouldn't need us."

Your contribution is valuable precisely because the work of change is challenging. Here I provide four tactics to keep going in the face of resistance as well as three character traits to combat resistance: *tenacity* in the face of rejection, *integrity* when tested by compromise, and *courage* in the face of what I call the drift. I'll share a story here about an obstacle that almost derailed my entire comeback effort. Resistance is part of realizing any vision. The vision-driven leader accepts this as part of the journey on the way to their desired future.

Question 9: Is it too late? Behind this question lurks the nagging feeling for some that the window has already closed on becoming a vision-driven leader. It hasn't, and I'll share two concepts to prove it: the Vision Arc and the Vision Zag. As companies like Marvel, LEGO, Amazon, Microsoft, and Slack show, it's never too late to launch a new and winning vision.

Question 10: Are you ready? The statistics on entrepreneurialism in this country are not encouraging at the moment. I like to think by the time you reach the end of our journey together, you'll have everything you need to ignite your inner JFK, become a vision-driven leader, and change those numbers for the better. I'll wrap up with five simple steps to help you succeed in developing and delivering a Vision Script that will help you and your organization thrive in a new and better future.

If you'd like a little extra help in drafting your Vision Script, I've created a free new interactive tool called the Vision Scripter to get clear on your vision, draft your Vision Script, and then share it with your team. It uses video coaching, questions, and cues to make writing a compelling vision simple and easy. Check it out at VisionDrivenLeader.com.

What's Your Moon Shot?

Do you have a vision that propels the trajectory of your company, a destination that energizes investors and employees alike? What about an exciting outcome that delights your customers? I'm not talking about increasing your sales by 3 percent year-over-year, nudging overhead downward, or repaving the parking lot. That's business as usual.

Vision is all about painting a picture of an irresistible future. You'll be on the right track if your vision is big and challenging enough to scare you a bit. It should. If it doesn't, it's probably too small. Moon shots are about changing the world, or at least your sphere of influence within it. And I'm confident your sphere is far larger than you currently realize. The sheer audacity of an inspiring vision is like a bolt of electricity, a shock to the system, one that fires up and harnesses the team's momentum to seize the future.

So, are you a leader or a manager? If you're a leader—or if you want to become one—and if you yearn to be equipped to create and cast a vision for your organization, then read on. You're a tenth of the way through already.

A vision is not a guarantee. Plenty of visions fail. But having no vision is a guarantee of failure. It's only a matter of time before stagnation or strategic failures rob you of your future. I know because I've experienced it firsthand. It's a story I'll share next in Question 2.

Jumpstart Your Vision Script

The Vision Scripter is a simple, interactive system
that makes crafting your Vision Script fast and easy.
Try it free at VisionDrivenLeader.com

What Difference Does Vision Make?

The Pitfalls of Vision-Deficit Leaders

You've got to be careful if you don't know where
you're going, 'cause you might not get there.

YOGI BERRA[1]

After early stints at two publishing houses, Word Publishing and Thomas Nelson, I was excited to start a house of my own. How hard could it be? I was just thirty-one years old, but my business partner, Robert Wolgemuth, and I knew we were ready. We were both optimistic, brash, driven, and filled with enough raw energy and ideas to light a small city.

What was our vision for this new operation? Both of us had seen publishers pass on acquiring great books, titles we thought were significant and meaningful. We figured all we had to do was get a piece of that action and we'd be golden. We were convinced we could make a difference in the world if we could discover uncut gems overlooked by the corporate giants.

That's about as much forethought as we gave to our business vision, and things went so well up front, we didn't know that was a problem until it was too late.

Home Run!

We published five titles in 1989, which was also the year of our first big break. In October 1988, the Los Angeles Dodgers had won the World Series. The next month, through a mutual friend, Robert and I landed an appointment with Orel Hershiser, the Dodgers' star pitcher.

We first met Orel, his wife, and his agent in Washington, DC, and had a very hopeful conversation. He seemed excited about the prospect of working with us. We then flew with our new friends to New York by private jet, where we had dinner together. Heady stuff for a couple of young turks from Nashville, Tennessee.

It was exciting, but of course the Big Apple meant we'd be competing for the book against New York publishers. We'd now be bidding against the biggest houses on the planet. They'd drive up the royalty advance for the book. We could only hope we'd made a favorable enough impression that Orel would publish with us in spite of the money.

In December, Orel's agent called us. "I have great news," he said. "Orel would like to publish his book with you, provided you're willing to pay a royalty advance of—" He gave us the dollar amount, which was north of big but still south of stupid. Without a moment's hesitation, Robert and I said,

"Absolutely. We're in!" We then promised to get him a contract the next day.

We hung up the phone and high-fived. "Only one problem," I said, my mind going back to the advance. "Where are we going to come up with the money?"

Robert laughed. "Oh, yeah," he said, "that!" Suddenly, we didn't know if we should celebrate or puke.

We called one of our investors, who also sat on our board. We shared with him our story of meeting Orel and his agent's decision to give us a chance to publish the book. "Way to go, guys," he said. "I'm proud of you!" We then explained the money problem.

"We're confident this book will be a bestseller, so we just need a short-term loan," we said. "Can you help us out?" We held our breath.

To our surprise, he said, "You bet, guys. This is going to be huge." We were elated. Then he added a proviso: "Just one thing I need you to do. As part of the loan agreement, I need you to pledge all the stock certificates for your company to me as collateral. If you're willing to do that, we can make this happen." He wasn't going to risk that kind of money unless we had skin in the game. We agreed.

We signed Orel to a publishing contract and produced his book in fewer than a hundred days. *Out of the Blue* debuted on the *New York Times* list on April 23, 1989, at number five and remained there for several weeks. We were able to repay our investor; he was thrilled. Our families were thrilled too, since we didn't need to give our business away and move out of our homes. It was one of those times when everything just worked.

And it wasn't only that time. Those first few years were incredible. We were publishing everything: nonfiction, fiction, children's books. We even started work on a Bible, an incredibly complicated project for a small house like ours. Was it smart to bite off that much or stretch that far? Who could say? Without a vision directing our strategy, we took whatever opportunities seemed good at the time. And that plan worked great—right up until it didn't.

Strikeout

By 1990 we had grown to forty-three frontlist titles, fourteen employees, and $5 million in annual revenue. Not bad for a lean, mean team with a sales force of three. That's when we started to imagine where our revenues would go if we could tap into a relationship with a big-time book distributor. More sales reps equals more sales, or so we thought.

We were convinced finding a major distribution partner would take us to the next level. Of course, without a vision in place, we had no way of defining what that "next level" was. All we knew was that our three sales reps were on pace to deliver $400,000 a month. We signed with a company that had twenty full-time reps, our former employer, Word Publishing. They agreed to take on distribution of our titles, and we figured we would at least double our numbers. We confidently laid off our own guys and buckled up for something big.

But it never came. In the first month, our new distributor delivered $40,000 in sales. A mistake, right? How could a sales force of that size sell a tenth of what we were doing on our own? The scope and complexity of our product line probably didn't help us. Whatever the problem, publishing is a very capital-intensive business, and shortfalls like that are catastrophic. We were on a pretty significant growth curve and needed to invest in inventory and royalty advances for new authors. We required our limited cash reserves to keep the presses rolling, cover payroll, sign new projects, and keep the lights on. We hit the panic button and scheduled an emergency call with one of the executives at our partner company.

"Don't sweat it," he reassured us. "I know it's a little bit slower than we anticipated, but it's going to be okay. The guys here are getting used to your products. You know, just part of the ramp-up. Everything's going to be cool next month."

"Let's hope so," we said. "We can't continue on this sales trajectory and survive. This will kill us!"

He had a stopgap. "Why don't we advance you what you need as a short-term loan against your future sales?" he offered. "We know the numbers are going to come. We'll just pay you in advance against those future sales." We took the lifeline.

Our distribution partner advanced us a couple hundred thousand dollars. It wasn't quite enough, but we delayed some payments, made it work, and hoped for the best. But the turnaround never materialized. The company delivered a check for $45,000 the next month, and over the next several months never exceeded $60,000.

Within a few short months, we were on the hook for $1.1 million in sales advances. To secure these loans, without which we would have gone belly-up thanks to the reduced sales volume, we had to pledge all of our assets—everything from publishing contracts to the office furniture—as collateral. And that was our undoing. Unbeknownst to us or them at the time, the owner of the company we'd partnered with, Capital Cities/ABC, was negotiating to sell the company.

My partner and I had **passion**. We had **drive**. We had ideas. We had **execution**. And we had **confidence** to spare. But none of that was enough to replace **vision**.

We finally got a phone call. "I don't know how to tell you guys this," our partner's CEO said, "but they're calling your loan to clean up our balance sheet."

They gave us thirty days to repay. There was no way. Our dream was over after four years. Robert and I were crushed. I still remember that day in April 1992 when an 18-wheeler pulled up to our offices in Brentwood, Tennessee, and took everything away. We didn't even have chairs left to sit in. We couldn't pay severances to our staff. We had to abandon projects, including one author's book that was on the presses and scheduled to print the day our doors closed.

When people ask me about that business failure, I say in retrospect, I'd never like to repeat it, but I wouldn't trade it for the world. Why? Some of the most valuable lessons I've learned in business came from that experience. One is the primary, foundational, rock-bottom importance of vision. In 1998 I returned to Thomas Nelson and advanced through the company on the strength of that insight, eventually becoming CEO and chairman. And as if to prove God has a sense of humor, Nelson was the same company that had bought Word just six years before.

Robert and I had passion. We had drive. We had ideas. We had execution. And we had confidence to spare. But none of that was enough to replace vision. Passion and the rest can fuel the mission, but vision is the North Star to get you there.

Six Pitfalls of Vision-Deficit Leaders

What difference does vision make? As I've studied the question, worked with entrepreneurs and executives, and led organizations myself, I've found that vision-*deficit* leaders trip headlong into one or more of six pitfalls: unpreparedness for the future; missed opportunities; scattered priorities; strategic missteps; wasted money, time, and talent; and premature exits. Let's look at each one at a time.

1. Unpreparedness for the future. While nobody can see the future, a vision can clarify the future and prepare a company for what is on the horizon. One of the best stories I know to illustrate the point starts back at the turn of the twentieth century.

Photographs were rare when George Eastman first started making cameras in the late 1800s. The bulky equipment and dangerous chemicals required expert users. As a result, the average person would "have their picture made" only once or twice during their entire lifetime. Eastman was determined to simplify photography, "to make the camera as convenient as the pencil."[2]

In 1900, Eastman and his company, Kodak, introduced the Brownie, a simple snapshot camera preloaded with film and the slogan "You push the button, we do the rest." Americans snatched up more than 250,000 units in the first year of production. Virtually overnight, Eastman's camera transformed the way the world captured and memorialized life. The "Kodak Moment" was born.

For the next ninety years, Kodak and its film dominated the photography market, commanding a 90 percent share. But Kodak became complacent and even antagonistic toward the vision of customer-first innovation that inspired their founder. The prime example is what eventually destroyed the company.

In 1975, long before the technology was on the radar of its competitors, a Kodak electrical engineer named Steven Sasson invented the first digital camera. Unfortunately, Kodak's leadership couldn't—or wouldn't—envision a future without film. They couldn't imagine a profitable business model outside of what already existed. "It was filmless photography," said Sasson, "so management's reaction was, 'that's cute—but don't tell anyone about it.'"[3]

When vice president Don Strickland advised going digital, company leadership shot him down. "We developed the world's first consumer digital camera and Kodak could have launched it in 1992," Strickland said. "We could not get approval to launch or sell it because of fear of the cannibalization of film."[4] Instead of revolutionizing their industry and following their founder's vision of convenient photography for the masses, Kodak suppressed the innovation within its own organization. As a result, it was unready for the tidal wave of innovation on the horizon. By the time Kodak had finally adopted the technology it pioneered, the future had already passed them by. And, as I'm sure you know, there's more to the story.

"There is no reason anyone would want a computer in their home." So said Ken Olsen, founder of Digital Equipment Corporation (DEC), in 1977.[5] By contrast, Apple founder Steve Jobs predicted, "The most compelling reason for most people to buy a computer for the home will be to link it into a nationwide communications network."[6] And Jobs made that statement four years before the invention of the World Wide Web.

Jobs's vision was not an inevitability. The only reliable foregone conclusion is that there are very few foregone conclusions. But as a vision-driven leader, Jobs was able to imagine and then prepare for the possibility. As a result, the home computer market was fertile territory for the future growth of Apple. Olsen was locked in the present, and his lack of vision meant DEC made no such preparation—and when was the last time you heard the name DEC?

I often come back to something Jobs's wife, Laurene Powell, said at his funeral in 2011: "It is hard enough to see what is already there, to remove the many impediments to a clear view of reality, but Steve's gift was even greater: he saw clearly what was not there, what could be there, what had to be there. . . . He imagined what reality lacked, and he set out to remedy it."[7]

Jobs saw that computing power was reserved primarily for large corporations and small businesses. But that reality was lacking, and he could sense it. So instead of simply imitating what IBM, Hewlett-Packard, Compaq, and Commodore were doing in the small-business space, Jobs looked further down the road. He saw that, as he said, "Computers will be essential in most homes,"[8] and he set out to create a "domesticated computer."[9] That's what reality lacked.

He did the same with the revolutionary introduction of the iPhone, which opted for a touch screen at a time when clunky-keyed Palm devices and BlackBerrys were all the rage. Which takes me back to Kodak.

As of 2017, an estimated 1.2 trillion digital photos are taken annually by more than a billion consumers equipped with smartphones, the ultimate convenience photography.[10] Whether it's posting a pic of a dancing cat, or capturing and preserving great emotional moments such as a wedding, the birth of a child, or a sporting triumph, we take more pictures in two minutes today than all the photos snapped during the first hundred years of film.[11]

Computer scientist Alan Kay is famous for saying, "The best way to predict the future is to invent it."[12] Vision is the first step in doing that. Without it, leaders are unprepared for whatever is coming next. Through Steve Jobs's iPhone, and the innovators and copycats who have followed in his footsteps, George Eastman's vision lives on. Meanwhile, the shutter has all but closed on Kodak.

2. Missed opportunities. Being unprepared for the future means overlooking key opportunities in the present. Why? Vision keeps us attuned to possibilities that align with the future we see. Without a vision, those opportunities slide right by.

In 1982, three former Texas Instruments executives saw an opening in the emerging technology market and, in eight short months, shipped the very first Compaq computer. I was an early adopter, one of many. Compaq broke the record for the "first year of sales of any company in American business history—$111 million."[13] The upstart became the fastest company in history to cross the $1 billion sales threshold.[14] By 1987, one in every six personal computers sold by dealers was a Compaq.[15] A decade later, their phenomenal growth made Compaq the "undisputed global leader of the PC industry," primarily selling to businesses.[16] And now?

The success of Compaq caused them to take their eyes off of the trends within the industry. They needed a fresh vision to sustain and grow their business, but instead of being future focused, they were stuck in the present. Rather than addressing changing consumer appetites, they doubled down on more of the same, acquiring Digital Equipment Corporation in 1998 for $9.6 billion instead.[17] And, sure enough, that's the same DEC mentioned in pitfall one above, which should tell you where this is going.

> **Vision keeps us attuned to possibilities that align with the future we see.**

While Compaq was busy metabolizing the DEC acquisition, Apple, Dell, and Gateway tapped into a hungry home-computer market, and Compaq pivoted too late. Three years later, Dell passed Compaq as the industry leader in PC sales.[18] Why did Compaq overlook the exploding direct-to-consumer home market? Looking back on their glory days, their vice president of North American marketing, Gian Carlo Bisone, said, "Growth is the worst deodorant. It hides a lot of things." Doing a bit of soul-searching of his own, Chief Financial Officer Daryl White admitted, "We only saw our own success."[19] Further complicating their situation after their merger with DEC was that "the combined company lacked direction."[20] Translation: they lacked a vision.

Contrast that story with Nick Swinmurn and Tony Hsieh's. In 1999, Swinmurn got the crazy idea of selling shoes online. Investors thought it would never fly. They imagined too many logistical and customer-service challenges. Besides, the opportunity seemed minuscule. At the time the nearest comparison was mail-order shoe sales, which was a measly 5 percent of the market. Not surprisingly, most investors wouldn't return his calls. But Hsieh heard something in Swinmurn's pitch that made his ears perk. The mail-order business was only 5 percent of the market—but that market was $40 billion!

If catalog sales were already two billion, the logistical and customer-service challenges must not be that big a deal. The market was potentially massive! So Hsieh invested, and Zappos was born. When he finally sold to Amazon a decade later, the company was worth $1.2 billion. Swinmurn gave the same pitch to everyone, but Hsieh looked at the facts with a different sense of what was possible. Vision allowed him to see an opportunity, where other investors saw only obstacles.

Many leaders focus on strategy, while some emphasize the company mission. All well and good, but if you overlook the contribution of vision, you won't get the results you desire.

3. Scattered priorities. Without a vision, the opposite is also a problem. When we're unclear about our destination, we tend to make short-range decisions, pursuing whatever opportunities look good in the moment. This was one of the prime mistakes my partner and I made with our publishing venture. As we painfully discovered, opportunities that appear promising up close can prove disastrous in wider perspective.

The innovative wearable tech company Jawbone was a Silicon Valley darling, underwritten by five top-tier venture capital firms. But all their funding was like giving a dog too much leash. With no clear vision of where they were going, they chased too many opportunities—trying one product after another—and blew through $900 million in funding before going belly-up.

Some observers blamed competition from more established firms. "The bluetooth headset-turned-speaker-turned-wearables maker faced stiff competition from the likes of Apple and Fitbit," one said.[21] But the more obvious problem is right at the start of the quote. Jawbone never figured out what it wanted to be when it grew up. No amount of money can save you without vision; this is especially true when you're cash-rich. It's tempting to believe you can pursue dozens of good opportunities and succeed at them all. But that's untrue.

The following headline came closer to the truth: "Jawbone's Demise a Case of 'Death by Overfunding' in Silicon Valley."[22] How could too much money be a problem? When it cushions you from deciding what you want the future to be. In the end, Jawbone will be remembered primarily as one of history's largest venture-backed duds.[23]

Scarcity forces us to ask what we really want, and that, as we'll see, is a critical question for vision-driven leaders. An abundance of resources can enable us in avoiding the hard work of getting clear on our vision.

It didn't have to end that way for Jawbone. As Apple has demonstrated, the winning formula is a relentless focus on creating a range of excellent products that surpass customer expectations and align with your vision. Less is more. Which is why Jobs was passionate about the power of saying no to opportunities that didn't line up with his vision. After the Apple product line had grown to 350 different offerings in Jobs's absence, Jobs slashed it to just ten when he returned in 1998.[24]

"People think focus means saying yes to the thing you've got to focus on," he famously said. "But that's not what it means at all. It means saying no to the hundred other good ideas that there are. You have to pick carefully. I'm actually as proud of the things we haven't done as the things I have done. Innovation is saying no to 1,000 things."[25] He went so far as to preach that message to then incoming Nike CEO, Mark Parker.

Parker, as the story goes, spoke on the phone with Jobs after taking the helm at Nike. He asked him if he had any advice. "Well," said Jobs, "just one thing. Nike makes some of the best products in the world. Products that you lust after. But you also make a lot of crap. Just get rid of the crappy stuff and focus on the good stuff."[26] The trouble is, in the moment, the crappy stuff usually looks decent, even good. But vision can help you separate the seemingly good from the legitimately great.

4. Strategic missteps. Here's a simple but powerful truth: The future hasn't happened yet. It's imaginary. It doesn't exist. And it can take one of countless shapes, depending on decisions we make in the present. Synthesizing the learning from the first three mistakes above, vision steers our decision-making in the present by preparing us for the future, helping us spot the right opportunities, and shielding us from the bad.

Vision, in other words, helps us avoid strategic missteps and failures. It's a fact I wish I had known when I started my indie publishing venture, and it's a fact on display in the stories of Kodak and Fujifilm. Both companies focused on selling and developing film. Both companies utilized chemicals and special papers to develop and print the end product. Both companies developed and aggressively marketed disposable

35mm cameras to a worldwide market. Both companies were riding high at the dawn of the digital revolution.[27] But Kodak went bankrupt while Fuji thrived.

Between 2000 and 2010, the film market plunged, dropping 20–30 percent per year. Kodak's vision deficit meant a lack of imagination and resourcefulness in responding to the crisis. As we saw, they were entirely unprepared for the future. With their best thinking they were able only to slow their demise.

Not so with Fujifilm, which found ways to diversify and thrive. In fact, while Kodak's sales fell by half, Fuji's revenue *grew* by more than the same percentage. As a vision-driven leader, the president of Fujifilm was prepared for what was coming. "A peak always conceals a treacherous valley," Fuji president Shigetaka Komori said back in 2001.[28]

Vision enabled Fujifilm to pivot on the crest of the downhill slope. Announcing a six-year plan called VISION 75, Komori ensured the company's technological strengths were redeployed into the arenas of pharmaceuticals and cosmetics. This was a radical departure from the apparent mission of the company, but a new direction was essential if the business was to survive the upheaval in the photography market. The company also predicted the meteoric rise of LCD screen technology and, leveraging their existing competencies, created protective LCD polarizer films for a market they now dominate.

When it came to digital imaging, Kodak had the biggest head start of all. Yet because they lacked vision, they were unable to pivot when it mattered. Two companies within the same business sector, both with access to the same intelligence on data and trends. One won. One lost. Their visions of the future differentiated their destinies.

5. Wasted money, time, and talent. When leaders focus on execution to the exclusion of vision, they miss the role vision plays in execution. As a result, they create frustration within their teams and waste valuable resources, including their own scarce time and energy.

Vision provides a direction for execution, as well as a standard by which to judge performance. Without it, teams invest themselves in irrelevant outcomes and unimportant projects. Beyond that, they don't even know if they're winning because there's no external standard to evaluate their progress. Everybody runs in circles. By aligning around a clear and compelling vision, you can avoid sideways energy and wasted effort. By minimizing or even eliminating the cross-purpose activities within your company, vision allows you to execute more effectively.

And our teams know this. In a survey of tens of thousands of employees, researchers asked, "What do you look for and admire in a leader (defined as someone whose direction you would willingly follow)?" Not surprisingly, honesty topped the list. But 72 percent said that the second-most-important requirement of a leader was that "he or she be forward-looking."[29] That response jumped to 88 percent for more senior positions. Our teams expect honesty from everyone they work with, but they especially want vision in their leaders. Without it, they experience frustration as they watch their efforts go to waste.

The trouble is that those teams don't see enough vision from their leaders. In her 360-degree assessment work, Herminia Ibarra found that leaders significantly overreport their competency with vision, compared to the opinion of those observing their performance. She called it "a notable gap."[30]

What's also notable is how much time and effort the leaders themselves waste when not following a vision. Researchers Heike Bruch and Sumantra Ghoshal studied two hundred Lufthansa managers. "Our findings on managerial behavior should frighten you," they reported. "Fully 90% of managers squander their time in all sorts of ineffective activities. . . . [A] mere 10% of managers spend their time in a committed, purposeful, and reflective manner." Forty percent—those they labeled "distracted"—were hyperbusy but disconnected from the organization's vision. As a result, they were shortsighted, overcommitted, and struggled to develop useful strategies. In other words, all their work amounted to less than it could have or should have. "They think they're attending to pressing matters, but they're really just spinning their wheels," said Bruch and Ghoshal.[31]

The right vision reminds people what we're building and why it matters. It inspires and energizes people across the organization by stirring within them the motivation to follow and do great things together. People can see how their actions contribute to the organization's vision.

That's what happened at NASA after Kennedy cast his vision to put a man on the moon. According to one report, "a strong connection between a NASA employee's day-to-day role and the ultimate goal" was made, as evidenced by this comment by a custodian: "I'm not mopping floors, I'm putting a man on the moon."[32]

6. Premature exits. All that wasted effort leads to frustration and futility, and that means vision-deficit leaders are prone to quitting the field early—same with their burned-out employees. The ultimate goal of a clear vision is to stay the course during the inevitable hurdles and resistance and succeed. Vision keeps you and your team motivated, engaged, and committed so you don't bail before the payoff. I can't think of a more compelling example of this dynamic than SwiftKey.

Three friends, Chris Hill-Scott, Jon Reynolds, and Ben Medlock, cofounded SwiftKey in 2008. Equipped with a simple vision of the future—"there had to be a better way of typing on smartphones"—they set off to create the best predictive text virtual keyboard app for Apple and Android mobile devices.[33] They envisioned and developed an AI-backed keyboard that "learned" how the customer communicated by tapping into the user's social media accounts. Their Prediction Engine gathered intel from Twitter and Facebook, as well as Evernote, Gmail, and the user's contact list. They launched the beta version after just two years.

Reviewers and users raved, and SwiftKey skyrocketed in popularity. They racked up more than a dozen industry awards during their first four years on the market, along with more than 300 million users. I'm one of them. Six years after launch, they estimated their market-leading keyboard technology had saved users "nearly 10 trillion keystrokes, across 100 languages, saving more than 100,000 years in combined typing time."[34] Too bad there's not a Nobel Prize for productivity. To cap off this story, Microsoft bought SwiftKey for $250 million in 2016.[35] The vision of these three founders paid off—mostly.

At the time of the Microsoft buyout, just two of the three original partners were still with the company to cash in. Why? Medlock and Reynolds kept the big picture in view. They pushed through the long hours associated with any startup and watched their dream unfold before their eyes.

Meanwhile, in what he now calls "the biggest mistake I ever made," Hill-Scott decided to withdraw from the company after just two months on the job.

According to published reports, he "grew tired of the long hours and work required."[36] I can't say with certainty, but my guess is that he lost his vision for what could have been if he had stayed the course. He was focused on the day-to-day drain rather than the big, inspiring picture. Because he cashed out early, instead of millions, he earned just enough to buy a bicycle.

When slowdowns and setbacks threaten to throw you off course, when breakthroughs remain elusive, vision can sustain the mission and lead you to your projected outcome. But only if you still have one.

Changing the Future

At the turn of the twentieth century, when the horse and buggy were the primary means of transportation for most people, Henry Ford had a vision that would define the future. When he introduced the Model T in 1908, Ford said that he wanted to "build a car for the great multitude. It will be large enough for the family but small enough for the individual to run and care for." That was a significant future-defining vision. It's reminiscent of George Eastman's original vision and just as compelling, if not more so.

At the time, automobile ownership was limited to the wealthy, "a plaything for the rich." A vehicle was so complicated to operate, it typically "required a chauffeur conversant with its individual mechanical nuances to drive it."[37] But Ford envisioned a dependable car that average Americans could afford—something that didn't exist at the time.

"It will be constructed of the best materials, by the best men to be hired, after the simplest designs that modern engineering can devise," Ford said. "But it will be so low in price that no man making a good salary will be unable to own one and enjoy with his family the blessing of hours of pleasure in God's great open spaces."[38] I love that. Who wouldn't? History is full of similar stories, where a change in vision resulted in a change in outcome. It's also full of stories like those recounted above, including my own, where a lack of vision resulted in ruin. That's the difference vision makes. If you're not convinced of the point, feel free to set this book down. But if you recognize the importance and want to craft a better vision for your future, keep reading.

In this book, my operating assumption is that, both in business and in life, you're much more likely to get to a destination that you're going to like if you're intentional about where you're heading. That's one of the reasons I view vision as the lifeblood of any organization. It keeps you moving forward. Vision serves as the engine to drive your company into the future. Vision provides meaning to the day-to-day challenges and setbacks that make up the rumble and tumble of real life along the way. And, as we saw with Kodak, Fujifilm, and other examples above, vision isn't a static thing. It can, should, and must change as goals are reached or as the industry changes.

Now that you understand the difference that vision makes in your organization, are you ready to create your own? That's what we'll do in part 2, as we answer five key questions, starting with, What do you want?

DRAFTING YOUR VISION SCRIPT

The soul never thinks without a mental image.

ARISTOTLE

Leadership comes when your hope and your optimism are matched with a concrete vision of the future and a way to get there.

SETH GODIN

Direction, not intention, determines destination.

ANDY STANLEY

What Do You Want?

Direction Begins with Desire

You should always take the best from the past, leave
the worst back there, and go forward into the future.

BOB DYLAN[1]

On May 25, 2001, thirty-three-year-old Erik Weihenmayer stood on top of the world. After three months
alternating between climbing and pausing to get acclimated
to the altitude, Erik, along with a group of eighteen other
mountaineers, summited Mount Everest. Ninety percent of
climbers who attempt the summit fail to make it.[2]

Climbing Everest is not for the faint of heart. Risks include crevasses, avalanches, frostbite, winds approaching
100 miles per hour, subzero temperatures, blizzards, earth-
quakes, dangerously low oxygen, high-altitude pulmonary
edema, and hypoxia. As of this writing, nearly 300 climbers
have died trying to reach the top since 1922.[3] Aware of the

risks, Weihenmayer's team battled the elements, injuries, dysentery, fevers, and more. But no risk was quite so daunting as this: Weihenmayer is blind.

As a young boy, Weihenmayer suffered from retinoschisis, a rare retina disease that progressively worsened until, at age thirteen, he was completely blind. But Weihenmayer didn't let his physical blindness get in the way of what he wanted out of life. At age twenty, he had a vision of scaling the Seven Summits—climbing the highest peaks on each of the seven continents.

> We all have mountains of our own, and vision is the only reliable path to the top.

Weihenmayer might have been blind, but he had incredible vision. When faced with what appear to be insurmountable odds, he never lost sight of what he wanted to accomplish. As a result, he became one of the first 150 people to scale the Seven Summits—the first and only blind person to do so.[4] "No one has ever done anything like it," *Time* magazine said of his accomplishments. "It is a unique achievement, one that in the truest sense pushes the limits of what man is capable of."[5]

Whatever the risks and odds, we all have mountains of our own, and vision is the only reliable path to the top. Leadership is not a gently sloping road. Oftentimes there is no road. It's only possessing a clear vision that enables leaders to make a way when none previously existed. It all comes down to what you want. Unless you're clear on that, you'll never stand a chance of achieving it.

So what do you want? We'll look at how a Vision Script can help you create a detailed answer to that question. We'll also examine what it takes to write one for your organization.

Not a Mission Statement

When answering Question 2, I told you my story of how lacking vision sank my business. Now, let me tell you the other half of the story—how vision saved the day in my next adventure. After several years working as an agent, I came back to work for Thomas Nelson in 1998 and became associate publisher for Nelson Books, one of the company's fourteen imprints, or business units. That meant I was second in command behind my boss, the publisher—who decided to quit in July 2000.

It's not hard to figure out why. Our division was in wretched shape. Most of us sensed our sorry condition from office gossip and other clues. But our boss wasn't forthcoming with the details. I had no idea how bad things were until he left. Here's what I found after digging into the numbers:

- We were the least profitable division in the entire company. We had actually lost money the previous year. People in the other divisions were mumbling about our poor performance and blamed us for pulling down the entire company's revenue metrics, which in turn, prevented others from receiving their annual performance bonuses.
- Revenue growth had been basically flat for three years. In addition, we had just lost our single biggest author to a competing publishing company. This made revenue growth unlikely, to say the least.
- As a percentage of revenue, our inventory and royalty advances were the highest in the company. In other words, we were the least efficient users of working capital. We were consuming enormous corporate

resources and providing virtually no return to our shareholders.

- We were publishing about 125 new titles a year with a team of just ten people. I know of publishing houses who tackle half those titles with twice the body count. Everyone was spread thin and overworked. The quality of our output showed it. We simply had too much to do.

- Just 20 percent of our titles were generating 80 percent of our revenues. Candidly, we had by far more "dogs" than "cash cows" (to reference the old Boston Consulting Group matrix).

All of this mattered a lot at the time for one simple reason: I inherited this mess. With my boss's exit, I was asked to fill his job, to be the publisher, the leader, the one responsible for taking us up the mountain. I told part of this story in my book *Free to Focus*, but I want to go deeper with it here to illustrate the value of vision, especially with the backdrop of my prior business failure.

I had two simultaneous feelings: (1) overwhelming pressure to succeed, to not fail again, and (2) excitement. The situation couldn't have been worse; we were dead last in every possible metric. That explained the overwhelming pressure. What about the excitement? It's funny to admit, but as the new divisional executive, I was in the best possible position. Odds were good I couldn't make it worse! And if I turned the division around, I would be a hero. But how?

A story like this helps create an important distinction. I'm often asked, "What's the difference between mission and vision?" At first blush, they seem similar. People often speak as if they're interchangeable building blocks of a successful business. They're connected, and both are essential for a business to succeed, but it's important to recognize they're distinct concepts serving different purposes.

Both mission and vision inform strategy but in different ways. Mission provides day-to-day clarity by defining the identity and scope of the business. Without a clear mission, you can easily drift off target and head into either too many directions, or the wrong direction. An effective mission statement keeps you on task by answering four questions:

1. Who are we?
2. Who do we serve?
3. What problem do we solve?
4. What transformation do we deliver?

The answers to these four questions define your identity, your clientele, and your answer to your customers' challenges, along with the results you produce. All good, all necessary. But beside the point when it comes to vision. When I took over Nelson Books, I didn't need a mission statement. I needed a whole new direction. And that's a key differentiator. A mission defines what a business is, a vision describes where it's going. Mission is here; vision is still out there. Mission is now; vision is next.

Becoming publisher was a long-term career goal for me. When I got my big chance and discovered the business unit was a disaster, I instinctively knew I needed a clear plan of action. The first step I took in reversing the fortunes of our division was asking myself what I wanted the future to look like for me and my team. Where did we

> **Mission is now; vision is next.**

want to take this thing? What did we really want? To get answers, I left on a private retreat and plotted a whole new direction.

THE MISSION-VISION DIFFERENTIAL

Mission	Vision
What	Where
Here	Out there
Now	Next
Brief	Robust

Scripting Tomorrow

An effective mission statement is tightly worded, sharply focused, and memorable. You should be able to boil it down to a couple of sentences. "It should fit on a T-shirt," as Peter Drucker once said.[6] I needed to script a new and better vision. For me then—and for you now—that deserved and required more than a T-shirt.

A proper Vision Script is not a tagline or a bumper sticker. It's a robust document, written in the present tense, that describes your future reality as if it were today. How far in the future? I recommend three to five years. You can go longer, but in my experience you'll find the biggest gains in the three-to-five window.

The trick is to step into the future and record what you see in four key areas of your business: your team, products, sales and marketing, and impact. I'll unpack each of these in a moment. Let me say that when I first did this exercise, my Vision Script was less developed than what I outline below. I've refined the process in the years since to make the Vision Script even more effective.

One thing is, however, 100 percent the same: answering the question of what I wanted for my business in the future. This is true for all of us when crafting a vision. As we examine the four aspects of team, products, sales and marketing, and impact below, I'll give you examples of our current Vision Script at Michael Hyatt & Co. Every statement about the future tells us how we're performing in the present and influences what we do next.

The future of your team. It's important to begin your Vision Script with your team. Why? Because your team makes everything else possible. The right team will enable you, as the leader, to focus on what you do best. They'll execute strategy, take care of your customers, and cultivate new ones. The right team will blow you away with their ideas, ambition, skills, and know-how.

So, what does the ideal team look like to you three years out? And how does your organization take care of them and cultivate a winning culture? This needs to be specific enough for anyone reading to visualize it for themselves. You want to convey enough detail that other people see what you see so together you can build it.

When you imagine your team three years out, what do you see, for instance, in terms of their talents, experience, and work-life balance? What do you provide in terms of benefits, work environment, and incentives? There are no right or wrong answers. It just comes down to what you want for your team.

Some examples from the Michael Hyatt & Co. Vision Script include these: "Our teammates live and breathe our core ideology. They possess impeccable character, extraordinary talent, and proven track records"; "Our employees experience reasonable autonomy, planning and executing their own work, without the impediment of overbearing management, stifling bureaucracy, or procedural red tape"; and "We encourage innovation and experimentation. If something doesn't work, we learn from it and move on."

The future of your products. What are the products or the services you offer? At Michael Hyatt & Co., our Vision Script says, "We create products that enable leaders to get the focus they need to win at work and succeed at life." From there we elaborate with additional details: "We create products that delight our customers, exceed their expectations, and deliver dramatic transformation."

Do we always accomplish that? Not always, not perfectly. But that's to be expected. Vision is about next, not now. It's about where you're going, not where you currently are. The future vision provides a measuring stick for the present, but it is, as we said in Question 1, *superior* to the present. By definition, you're not there yet.

And that's where the excitement comes in! What's next in terms of your products? What do you want to create? What do you want to offer? Remember I mentioned that mission and vision are connected? A helpful tip for thinking through future products is to ask what you could create that would help you fulfill your mission.

Our vision for our products included statements like these: "Our ultimate product is not our information and tools but the transformation our clients and customers experience when using them"; "We employ a rigorous decision-making process to weigh necessary investment against our core ideology and projected ROI. As a result, we routinely say no to distractions masquerading as opportunities";

and "We employ a stable of talented coaches, speakers, podcasters."

The future of your sales and marketing. How do you get those amazing products to market? We're not talking nuts-and-bolts methods and strategies. This is a chance to think broadly and philosophically about your sales and marketing. It should be more than impressions and conversions (though include if helpful). This is fundamentally about how you relate to your customers.

At our company, we say, "We employ customer acquisition strategies that make our offers irresistible." Then we build upon that with other statements: "We understand that our clients and customers are the real heroes. We serve as a guide offering a plan that helps them overcome their obstacles and achieve their desired transformation"; and "We see world-class, hospitality-inspired customer experience as an essential marketing activity."

The future of your impact. Finally, your Vision Script should describe the intended outcome of the team's effort. What's the result of your realizing your vision? You can answer in terms of financial impact, but it can also be in other, less concrete ways, such as reach or influence or something less material.

In this last domain of our company's script, we start by saying, "As a result, we are transforming our world and achieving outstanding results." From there we cover the operational status of our principals, key financial metrics, team turnover rate, and this final nonnegotiable: "We have achieved these extraordinary results without compromising our values or culture."

FOUR KEY COMPONENTS
OF A VISION SCRIPT

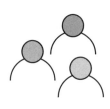
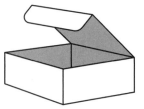

TEAM   **PRODUCT**

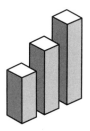

SALES &   **IMPACT**
MARKETING

These are the four key elements of a Vision Script, but your business
might require you to plan in additional domains. No worries. Just add
the categories you need to make your future work for you.

Before we move on, let's answer this question: "What if
my business is driven by something unaddressed in these
four areas?" There may be instances where that's the case. If
so, go ahead and add another domain to your Vision Script.
For example, if your business is capital intensive, you may
want to develop a statement around finance. If you lead a

nonprofit, you may need to add the area of donor relations. Just beware of adding too many areas to the statement. Each one must be essential to your business. Also, don't delete any of the four key areas. All are essential. Even if you're a solopreneur, your vision should include the development of a team. Without a team, a product, a market, and impact, you don't really have a business.

How to Write Your Own

As you consider writing your own vision, it's useful to admit upfront that this can be challenging. There are a handful of reasons. Sometimes, we're so absorbed in the day-to-day that it's tough to come up with a compelling vision for the future.

Other times, we feel as though we're just not that imaginative. But I don't buy it. It's not that we lack imagination—it's that we lack attention. Any leader who dedicates time and focus can draft a compelling vision for the future by simply asking themselves what they want and sticking with it until answers begin to emerge.

Humans are future-oriented unlike any other creature on this planet. While other animals have limited horizons, humans make and act on long-term plans all the time. In fact, says psychologist Martin Seligman, "a more apt name for our species would be *Homo prospectus*, because we thrive by considering our prospects."[7] Don't we know this from simple experience? All of us imagine the future constantly, if for no other reason than to worry about it. Let that work in your favor. All I'm asking is that you not conjure everything that could go wrong. Imagine if things went right.

Below are three tips for creating your own Vision Script. I'll share how these helped me craft my initial Vision Script for Nelson Books. As a reminder, you're trying to paint an inspiring, clear, practical, and attractive picture of your organization's future. Nothing else. Avoid, as career strategist Jenny Blake calls it, "the tyranny of the hows."[8] Just as this process is not about defining mission, it's also not about setting strategy. Later in Question 6, I'll explain how your Vision Script informs strategy.

1. Get away and clear your head. The future doesn't happen in the present, and it's hard, if not impossible, to craft a Vision Script in the midst of the day-to-day. It's important to step outside the whirlwind so you can see beyond the whirlwind.

In my case, I somehow knew formulating a vision for my division wouldn't happen amid daily tasks and projects. I knew the only way I could get clear was to get alone with my own thoughts, so I carved out time for a personal retreat.

In order to have the mental space to see your current reality and to envision what the future could look like, I recommend finding a solitary place away from the office: a hotel, retreat center, Airbnb, back corner of a public library, or even a coffee shop with your earbuds locked tight. Anywhere works as long as you won't be interrupted. Something remarkable happens when you unplug from the constant noise, distraction, and pace of life to think, ponder, and get in touch with your own thoughts. If it helps you, pray as you begin.

If at all possible, keep yourself from "touching base" with your office even after hours. Turn off your notifications. Write everything longhand on a legal pad if that's what it takes to stay disconnected. Like a black hole, the gravitational pull of email or Slack will suck you into a headspace that will compete with your efforts to achieve the mental space for vision.

2. Believe the best is yet to come. The future is all about possibility. Unfortunately, experience usually trains us to focus on what's not possible. We're conditioned to think about limits, constraints, and all the reasons our hopes are out of reach. And often, we're right.

But here's the dirty secret. It's a self-fulfilling prophecy. We tend to experience what we expect. That means the biggest barriers you and I face in life are often the ones living inside our heads. We create the fence that blocks our progress— not always, but more often than we'd probably care or dare to admit.

It's important to wrestle with this because part of creating a new vision for the future is being honest about the past and present and how they're influencing our view of what's possible in the future. We have to manage two feats at once: total honesty about our experience so far, and commitment to the idea that it can be better, even far better.

When I went on my vision retreat, I brought with me a number of spreadsheets, the last twelve months' profit and loss statements, our author roster, the organizational chart, and a SWOT (Strengths, Weaknesses, Opportunities, Threats) analysis. By the time I was done reading, I couldn't stop Bob Dylan's "Everything Is Broken" from playing in my head. Honestly, it would have been easy to assume the situation couldn't improve. The odds were against us, that's for sure. Compounding that reality, there was my own business failure looming in the background. I already sank one publishing company. How did I know I wouldn't finish off this division?

There's a famous basketball story that can help us here. In 1978, a fifteen-year-old sophomore and some fifty other student hopefuls filed into the Emsley A. Laney High School

The biggest **barriers** you and I face in life are often the ones living inside our **heads.**

gym with the dream of claiming one of fifteen spots on the varsity team. At the time, the boy was only 5'10" and couldn't keep up with the other boys. He didn't make the cut. "It was embarrassing not making the team," he admitted.[9] When he got home he went straight to his room, locked the door, and cried.

In the throes of disappointment, the boy could have said, "I'm not good enough. I'll never amount to anything on the court. There are just too many other players who are taller, faster, and better than I'll ever be." At that moment, his experience would have ratified that opinion. But instead of allowing limiting beliefs to shape his reality, he redoubled his efforts, driven to change his future.

"Whenever I was working out and got tired and figured I ought to stop, I'd close my eyes and see that list in the locker room without my name on it," he said, describing how he changed his mindset. "That usually got me going again."[10]

It paid off. As soon as I tell you that boy's name—Michael Jordan—you know the rest of the story. During his illustrious NBA career, Jordan scored 32,292 points. He appeared in fourteen All-Star games, nabbed six NBA championships, and was awarded the NBA MVP title five times.

History's full of stories where a change in thinking resulted in a change in outcome. Walt Disney was fired from his job at the *Kansas City Star* newspaper. Why? His editor said he "lacked imagination and had no good ideas."[11] When Oprah Winfrey was fired from her role as a TV reporter, the producer "reportedly told her she was 'unfit for television news.'"[12] Steven Spielberg was rejected from the University of Southern California film school three times. Rather than assume he didn't have the chops, he didn't abandon his vision of making compelling movies.

He went on to direct more than fifty films, including three Oscar-winners.[13]

And don't forget Erik Weihenmayer, whose story we started with. If anyone could have taken their present reality and allowed it to limit their future, it's him. But no. He wouldn't let anything hold him back from dreaming and achieving the seemingly impossible.

Experience—even bad experience—is just information. How you interpret and apply that information is up to you. You can use it to create limiting beliefs about what's possible, or you can embrace one simple liberating truth: whatever's behind you, the best is yet to come. And what is to come?

3. Imagine tomorrow and describe what you see. The final step in writing your Vision Script is imagining your future and describing what you see. Think of yourself as standing in the future. What do you see there? What does it look like?

This is not prediction or prophecy. There's nothing inevitable about it.[14] You're describing one of countless possible futures that will require the best thinking and effort of you and your team to realize. The future takes the shape of choices in the present. The idea is to imagine a tomorrow compelling enough to guide your choices today.

When describing this future, you want to write in the present tense, as though your vision has already happened. Here are some examples from my Nelson Books Vision Script: "Nelson Books publishes seven *New York Times* bestsellers per year"; "We sell ten books that sell over 100,000 units per year"; "We have great relationships with authors and agents"; and "We have a staff of extremely talented, extremely committed people."

To help me get started, I asked myself a number of probing questions, including:

- "What needs to change in our business model so that my team doesn't burn out or leave?"
- "What kind of authors and mix of titles do we need to attract to minimize the churn and maximize our profitability?" You can adapt that question for your own products and services.
- "How would our organization stack up against our competitors in the marketplace?"
- "What kind of innovations or processes could we invent that would help us scale our vision faster?"

There are many other questions that can help as well. Journalist Warren Berger shares a provocative question used by business consultant Don Derosby: "If an oracle could tell you what's going to happen three years from now, what would you most want to know?" The trick in the question is it reveals what interests, concerns, and excites you. No one knows the future, but, as Berger says, "the purpose of the question is to encourage one to focus on that future scenario. . . . Once you've thought of questions for the oracle, you must try to do the oracle's job of answering them."[15] Your answers become the start of your vision.

Berger suggests several other helpful questions culled from visioneering experts:

- "How can we become the company that would put us out of business?" and "What might this predator look like and why would it have an advantage over us?" (Danny Meyer, New York restaurateur, CEO of Union Square Hospitality Group)

- "Who do we want our customers to become?" (Michael Schrage, MIT professor)
- "Who are you spending time with? On what topics? Where are you traveling? What are you reading?" (Roselinde Torres, Boston Consulting Group)[16]

The last bullet assumes your interests can expose possible trends and point you to a desirable future. It also helps by connecting your future prospects to your current preoccupations, which is often where vision lurks. And it suggests something critical: a vision should be something that personally interests and motivates you. Let your curiosity pull you along—that's what it's for.[17] All of the above questions can put you in an imaginative headspace, one where tomorrow can take definitive shape in your mind. That's the essence of crafting a Vision Script for yourself.

To further help you with crafting your own vision, I've included several category-specific questions in the adjoining box.

I've also created an interactive version of these prompts. As I mentioned in Question 1, it's a tool called the Vision Scripter. It will guide you point by point through the process of drafting your Vision Script. When you're ready to create your vision, go to VisionDrivenLeader.com to try it out.

As you describe your ideal future, provide enough detail to make it concrete, using specific statements so people get a sense of what it is you're trying to build. Unless you can describe it, the team can't build it, and they won't know if they've built it when they're done. Using metaphors and stories in your Vision Script is fine, but don't lose sight of

Questions for Prompting Vision

If you could jump ahead three to five years and answer these questions, what would your answers include? Your answers can serve as the basis for your Vision Script.

Team

- What kind of teammates do you want to attract? What characteristics do they all share in common?
- How do they work? What is their work ethic?
- What do you do to attract top talent? What is your compensation philosophy? What does your benefits package look like?
- Why are prospective employees attracted to your company? What makes people beg to join your company?
- What does your office environment look like? Why does that matter to you?

Products

- What results do your products create? What value do they deliver?
- Who do your products help?
- How do your customers feel when they use your products? What's the user experience like?
- What does your production-creation process look like? How do you choose what to offer?
- What makes your products superior to those of your competitors?

Sales and Marketing

- What markets do you serve? How large is your customer base?
- How do you reach them?
- How much does it cost you to acquire new customers? What's your cost per lead?
- What's the lifetime value of your customer?
- How do you see your marketing, sales, and customer experience teams operating? What's their role in customer acquisition and retention?

Impact

- What are your results—by whatever metrics are most meaningful to you and your team? For instance, what's your revenue, your profit, staff count, or the size of your mailing list?
- What financial thresholds excite you as the leader?
- What are you, as the leader, free to do with your time and role?
- How do you hope that growth in your organization will impact you and your team?
- How do your industry peers and competitors think of you?

boiling those inspirational concepts down to concrete statements. By making your vision concrete, you're making it tangible and attainable. But remember, don't get hung up on how you will accomplish your vision. That comes later.

Feel free to customize this plan as necessary. As I said before, you may need additional components beyond the four I recommend. Go ahead and add them.

It's also worth saying that the complexity of your business might require you to look out farther than three to five years. When the toy company LEGO was on the brink of disaster, they employed a seven-year vision divided into three phases to come through the crisis.[18] The guidelines above are just that, guidelines; tweak as needed.

The Turnaround

Once I had captured my vision on paper, I came back to the office and called a meeting with my entire staff. I reviewed our current reality. I was brutally honest. The situation was dire, and I didn't pull any punches. (We'll discuss the best way to handle this conversation in Question 7.)

I then shared the new reality—the vision—and described it in as much detail as I could. I was genuinely enthusiastic and committed. Because I found the vision compelling, most of them did too. Some were slow to get on board, but in the end, even the most reluctant ones came around.

I personally read through this vision daily. I prayed over every part. I asked God to guide us. Little by little, the strategy and the resources emerged. People would ask me, "How in the world are you going to accomplish this?" I would just smile and say, "I'm not sure, but I am confident it is going to happen. Just watch."

When you're clear on what you want, you avoid the pitfalls of vision-deficit leaders. You're better prepared for the future. You capitalize on key opportunities because you're better attuned to what will help you move forward. Simultaneously, you tend to filter out opportunities that will distract or derail you.

Instead of strategy being ad hoc and determined by the needs of the moment, your strategy is aligned with your endgame. Because of that focus and alignment, you waste less money, time, and talent; your team is on board and pulling the same direction.

Finally, you're motivated to stick with it when the times get tough, and they will (more on that in Question 8). This is why I say vision is the essential ingredient in leadership. Only with vision do leaders have a fighting chance of making a difference. And in the case of Nelson Books, it made all the difference.

I thought my initial vision would take at least three years to accomplish. Amazingly, we got there in just eighteen months. We exceeded almost every aspect of our vision. It was a complete turnaround. Over the next six years, Nelson Books was consistently the fastest growing, most profitable division at Thomas Nelson. We had one bestseller after another. In fact, we were home to almost all of our company's bestselling authors during that season.

Comparing my prior business failure to this resounding success, I know vision made all the difference.

Qualifying Questions

Your Vision Script sets the course for your company's future win. That's why it's imperative to bring your full attention to this process by getting alone, believing the future can be better than your past and present experiences, and describing a new and superior future.

The next several questions will help you dial in your Vision Script, ensuring it's clear, inspiring, and attractive to the key stakeholders in your organization. You'll know you have something if you can sell it to your team. A vision-driven leader makes their vision come alive for others so they are not only inspired but also directed to act. Make your vision concrete and compelling, and others will join you in making it a reality.

That said, you're not Moses coming down from Mount Sinai with tablets of stone.[19] For now, think of your Vision Script as wet cement. As we'll see in Question 7, there's room for input and fine-tuning from your colleagues. Let's first refine your Vision Script so it's inspiring, clear, and practical; that will ensure your best chance in getting them on board. That's what we'll cover with the next three qualifying questions, starting with this one: Is it clear?

YOUR VISION SCRIPT

Every Vision Script looks different depending on the leader who creates it. You might write yours as a detailed narrative or just a list of bullets. Write your Vision Script in whatever style (1) flows most naturally and (2) helps you best envision your desired future for your team, product, sales and marketing, impact, and any other domain you require. The Vision Scripter at VisionDrivenLeader.com can help you draft a vision that works for you.

Is It Clear?

Make It Concrete and Explicit

A good leader thinks in shades of gray . . . but speaks in black and white.

BEAU LOTTO[1]

Back in junior high, I was dead set on being an astronaut. As I mentioned in Question 1, Tom Swift books triggered my interest in, and love of, science, tech, and space travel. Science fiction writers like Arthur C. Clarke and Robert Heinlein ramped up my passion for life among the stars. And, of course, so did President Kennedy's vision of putting a man on the moon. There was just one problem.

I still remember that fateful day at school when a friend said, "Mike, don't you know that to be a pilot you have to have perfect vision?" I was crestfallen. I felt in that moment as if my whole life was over. My eyeglasses were as thick as Coke-bottle bottoms. As soon as was possible, I made the switch from glasses to contact lenses, which I wore for most of my life, even after I traded the Pleiades for publishing.

But contacts weren't the complete answer. It turns out severely nearsighted people like me develop cataracts faster than the average person, so several years ago I made the decision to undergo lens replacement surgery.

The optical team conducted the procedure while I was almost fully awake. They gave me a sedative and then, using a series of anesthetic drops, numbed my left eye. (They do only one at a time, separating the surgeries by a couple of weeks.) Using a laser-guided machine, the doctor made a flap-like incision in my eye, removed the old lens, inserted a new artificial lens in its place, and made one stitch to secure the flap. Presto! The operation took less than fifteen minutes, and the results were immediate.

When I woke up in the middle of the night after the surgery, I was startled. The first thing I noticed when I opened my good eye were the brilliant colors and crystal clarity of vision. By comparison, my eyesight in the uncorrected eye was like looking through a window that hadn't been washed in years.

Thanks to the procedure, I could see across the room. Once I had the other eye corrected, I could go golfing without glasses. I could drive without contacts. Prior to that, I couldn't see the clock three feet from my pillow. Best of all, everything I viewed was sharper, more focused, and more vibrant than anything I'd seen in years.

What's more, I experienced something completely unexpected: a mood elevation. I didn't realize I was carrying around an undercurrent of stress because I couldn't see clearly. Clarity breeds calm. It also breeds confidence.

There's a useful parallel here to the way vision influences our organizations. Just as new lenses add clarity of vision and the accompanying sense of well-being, the same dynamic occurs when a vision-driven leader replaces the aimless business as usual with a vivid picture of the future. And that's why the first qualifying question for your Vision Script involves clarity.

Vision Requires Clarity

Think about what we expect from documents such as these:

- Affidavits
- Blueprints
- Book proposals
- Business plans
- College application guidelines
- Contracts
- Design briefs
- Device specifications
- Directions
- Employee handbooks
- Instructions
- Invoices
- Job descriptions
- Laws
- Legal briefs
- Marketing plans
- Product features
- Project estimates
- Recipes
- Safety protocols

The reason we insist these and similar documents are clear is because we expect them to serve certain ends, to produce particular results. And we judge their purported clarity based on whether we can use them to produce those desired results. If a recipe doesn't work, it's usually because something was unclear in the instructions. (Unless I'm cooking, in which case it's safe to blame user error.)

Vision is no different. But clarity can be hard to come by. Why? There's a tendency for visions to be abstract at first. We are, after all, describing the unseen, the not-yet-here, what lies over the horizon. But your Vision Script needs to be as clear, in its own way, as any of the documents listed above.

An unclear vision will not produce the results you're after. As professors Heiki Bruch and Bernd Vogel ask, "If you cannot clearly identify a vision in the first place and it remains in the realm of vague generalities, how can you hope to communicate it throughout the company?"[2] For a vision to be clear, it has to be concrete, not abstract.

But that's not all. Your vision must also be explicit. That is, it must be sufficiently expressed in easy-to-understand language. Because the vision usually starts with the leader, there's also a tendency for visions to live in their heads and never make it out. One reason is what's sometimes called the "curse of knowledge." The vision is obvious to the leader, because they know it, and so they assume everyone else knows it too—but how could others know it unless the leader shares the full picture?

A couple of years ago, some friends came in from California to meet with me for dinner. I went to the restaurant where we had agreed to meet in Franklin, which is just south of Nashville. A few minutes after five o'clock, I looked at my watch and thought, *Well, that's not like them. They're normally punctual.* The minutes crept by. I sat there five, fifteen, thirty minutes before I finally got a phone call.

"So sorry we're late, Michael," they said, sounding harried and embarrassed. "We're having difficulty finding the restaurant."

"Okay," I said. "No problem. It's right off of I-65. It's in Franklin, Tennessee. All you do is go south on I-65 from your hotel by the airport."

"Whoa!" they said. "We're in Franklin, Kentucky!" A simple mistake. They had punched "Franklin" into the GPS, and a "Franklin" popped up. They had driven straight north to Franklin, Kentucky, instead of straight south to Franklin, Tennessee. I had neglected to give them the full picture of where we were meeting. Since they were from out of town, how could they know?

Don't make the mistake of thinking your vision is obvious to the rest of the team just because you've shared it. I've learned the hard way that the direction and the needed steps may be clear to you, but that doesn't mean those around you will see things exactly as you do. A clear vision is not only concrete, it's also explicit. An implicit vision won't work well, if at all. If you or your team is unclear about the destination, you're going to wander.

> A clear vision is not only concrete, it's also explicit.

Maybe you've wondered why your company scrambles to gain traction on your vision for the future. Could it be that you have only a rough idea of where you'd like to lead the organization in the next three to five years? Have you made it as clear as a blueprint? Or are you using generic phrases to describe your big idea? Have you resisted carving out the time to sharpen your vision, leaving your employees confused?

When you provide a concrete, explicit vision for your team, you enable them to move faster in the right direction, full of purpose and confidence. Conversely, when you lack clarity, you're not going to make the same kind of progress.

Stress becomes an underlying byproduct. So do inefficiency, wasted resources, loss of time, and a demoralized team.[3]

Vision is about shared sight. It's not enough to see the future. You have to ensure others can see what you see and act on it. You don't drift to a destination you would have chosen. Instead, you have to be intentional, forcing yourself to get clear on what you want and then rendering it in a form that's both concrete and explicit. Thankfully, the Vision Grid can help us with that.

The Vision Grid

As an executive and executive coach, I've seen case after case where leaders struggle to transfer their vision to their team. Maybe they don't articulate it fully, leaving some of it unexpressed. Or they express it fully but use vague phrases and meaningless buzzwords. Some leaders who really struggle here might leave their vision both vague and unexpressed. Any of these three scenarios will end up frustrating everyone involved, rather than motivating productive action.

All three of these scenarios are the result of miscommunication. The Vision Grid is a tool that allows you to check your vision against four properties, whether it's abstract or concrete, implicit or explicit.[4] After you've taken a moment to study the grid, let's examine what goes on in each of the quadrants.

In *Quadrant 1* (abstract, implicit), the leader has a vague idea of what he wants the future to look like. It's more of a hunch, maybe wishful thinking. Since the picture in his mind is fuzzy, he fumbles for the right words to sell his vision; he never completely externalizes it. The team ends

THE VISION GRID

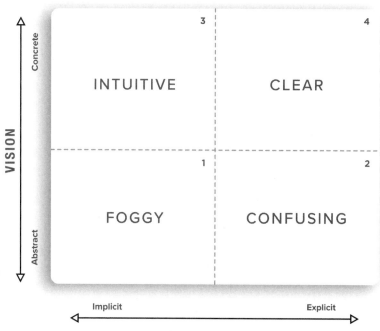

up in the Land of Foggy Thinking. As a result, the leadership is frustrated that the team is not going along with the program. But can you blame them? They don't know what direction to go.

In *Quadrant 2* (abstract, explicit), the leader also has a vague idea of what the future of the company might be. But rather than spend the necessary time to refine her vision, she speaks in definitive terms as she describes what to everyone else sounds like nebulous ideas. Often this happens when the leader is enthusiastic and effusive but hasn't translated that energy to language the team can connect with. She talks about synergy, going to another level, disruption, low-hanging fruit, and wheelhouses. Team members leave in a state of confusion. Some may think they know where the boss wants to take the company. Others leave feeling the emperor has no clothes.

In *Quadrant 3* (concrete, implicit), the leader has a fully developed, concrete vision of the future mapped out. He might even see all the necessary steps to move the team forward. But rather than be explicit and communicate the framework to the team, he wrongly assumes the vision ought to be obvious to his team. An intuitive vision can sometimes work in a small shop; in fact, it's common in startups. But the bigger the business gets, the more explicit the communication must be for the vision to register. Otherwise, what's obvious to the leader will be opaque to the team.

You're in trouble if your vision lives in any of these three quadrants. At various times, my failed publishing venture lived in one or another of these three. It was part of what sank our ship. Your team can't read your mind. Nor can they be clearer on your vision than you are. That's a recipe for confusion and frustration.

The situation improves dramatically, however, as we move into *Quadrant 4* (concrete, explicit), which is what a well-written Vision Script can help you do. In Quadrant 4, the leader has a fully developed, concrete vision of the future. She has fully detailed it for her team, articulating it in precise, unambiguous language. This kind of clarity allows her team to translate her vision into strategies, goals, objectives, and tasks. More than that, they can get a sense of the passion and purpose behind it all. Clarity creates connection. And there's nothing more satisfying than proceeding with confidence, knowing your team is aligned and passionate about the future because your vision is clear.

There's nothing more satisfying than proceeding with confidence, knowing your team is aligned and passionate about the future because your vision is clear.

So how do you gain clarity? Here are some tips I've found helpful and that have helped leaders I've worked with.

Five Steps to Gain Clarity

Early in my career I attended a sales conference in Colorado Springs while my wife, Gail, visited her parents in Denver. The plan was for me to join her after the event was over since Denver is not far from the Springs. That's when the unforeseen happened. Not long after I started north on I-25 to Denver, the moody, unpredictable Colorado weather went from sunny to snowy in a matter of minutes. The temperatures plunged while the snow started piling up.

When I reached the Black Forest Divide Pass—what's known as Monument Hill—the winds kicked in and deteriorated the visibility to maybe twenty feet. Here I was, a twenty-eight-year-old kid from Tennessee—originally raised in Waco, Texas—who rarely saw snow, let alone blizzard conditions. To say that I was scared would be an understatement. I was completely disoriented by the sudden whiteout.

That's when I noticed I was running low on gas. I inched off the nearest exit ramp in hopes of finding fuel. This was back in the days before cell phones with travel apps to direct you to the nearest station. Unfortunately, there wasn't fuel to be found at that exit. And, without a GPS to guide me, I got totally turned around. I didn't know which way to go to get back on the freeway to Denver. I couldn't see the street because everything was just a field of white.

I started debating whether I should stop the car and try to ride out the storm or press on. I didn't have any blankets and, with limited gas, I couldn't leave the engine running to stay warm. Plus, I didn't have food or water. I sat there trying to calculate the risk. If I stayed, I could freeze to death. But if I continued, I could run off the road—and freeze to death. The only thing I was clear on was that I had to make a decision. Figuring that anywhere had to be better than where I was at the moment, I pressed on, crawling at a snail's pace of maybe twenty-five miles per hour on a road with a speed limit of seventy-five miles per hour. Thankfully, I found my way north, found an open gas station, and made the trip in about six nail-biting hours. Without the adverse weather, I could have made the trip in ninety minutes tops.

The clearer you are, the faster and more reliably you go. Conversely, the fuzzier things are, the slower and more uncertain you move. Without clarity, navigating your path in life and in business is like driving in a blizzard. You might ultimately reach your destination, as I did, but clarity of direction significantly enables your ability to get there fast. As Jenny Blake says, "The clearer your vision, the easier it will be to decide what next steps to take and the stronger your instincts will become along the way."[5]

So how do you get clear when you feel fuzzy? Maybe you're unsure about your plan, you're not sure what to do, and it looks like your competition is flying by, leaving you in the dust. Every leader faces this at one time or another. In fact, one of the top three challenges leaders face, according to an informal survey of MichaelHyatt.com readers, is not having enough clarity to accomplish our vision and goals. So how can we find the clarity we need? It's simpler than you might think. Here are five simple steps to gain clarity and move forward.

First, *admit you're unclear*. It's easy to deny when we're directionless. We want to project confidence even when we don't feel it. So it's hard to admit we're missing something.

But that's the first step toward clarity: admitting we don't have it. Until then, we're not ready for it.

Second, *recognize your blinders.* In her book *Clarity First,* Karen Martin identifies six key factors that keep leaders unclear. They're all different, but they work to cloud the world around us: ignorance, lack of curiosity, overconfidence, cognitive biases, time constraints, and fear.[6] It takes some self-reflection to see if any of these are operative, but it's worth the effort.

Third, *ask for input.* I am a firm believer in the proverb "Without counsel plans fail, but with many advisers they succeed."[7] There are many sources of good counsel: spouses, mentors, executive coaches, business colleagues, industry peers, your team, and so on. Ask them what they think. You're not alone.

Fourth, *process the feedback.* Now that you have feedback from the sources that matter most, you need to process it. I suggest getting alone, reflecting, and journaling. Writing externalizes our thoughts, which helps us critique and improve them. I also strongly suggest including core members of your team. Review the work together.

Fifth, *just start.* It's important to get moving. When you can't read a sign, you have several options: think more about what the sign might say, scrunch up your eyes to change your focus, buy high-powered glasses, or ask a friend to read it to you. But the best and easiest way to get more clarity is to just move closer to the sign. Taking steps forward can bring things into focus.

And that's true for your Vision Script. Blake offers the same basic advice when people tell her they're unclear on their vision. "I never accept 'I don't know' as an answer," she says. "Because every time (and I do mean *every* time) I follow up with: 'Guess. Just take a stab at it, even if you don't know specifics,' answers start pouring out. 'I don't know' quickly dissolves after further inquiry."[8] So just start. Don't expect the vision to come into focus instantaneously, like some blinding flash of revelation. It probably won't. Martin compares clarity to a habit, which

> Vision is not a once-and-done phenomenon. It's a process.

takes time to develop. "Patient persistence is key," she says.[9]

The good news is that we don't have to see the whole thing at once, and we can avoid wasting a lot of time and worry trying. Vision is not a once-and-done phenomenon. It's a process. Remember, at this point your Vision Script is still wet cement. As you start working toward your vision, those initial steps will help you make it more concrete and explicit.

We all find ourselves lost on the roadside from time to time or moving with only a vague sense of where we're going. These five steps can give us the direction we need to find the right course and reach our goals and vision.

The Road Ahead

So, is your vision clear? As a vision-driven leader, you are your organization's eyes into the future, driving its performance down a pioneering path. In order to be an effective leader, a clear vision is needed so that your organization has the best opportunity to survive and thrive. Because a company can accelerate its rise with the right vision, and a company can avoid decline with the right vision.

When I say "the right vision" I'm referring to a vision that not only addresses what you want (Question 3) but that is also concrete and explicit. When you have reached that level of clarity, the team knows where you're going, and they're inspired to follow you into the future reality.

Clarity without inspiration leads to boredom and disinterest, and inspiration without clarity leads to excitement without direction. Your vision has to include both. That's why inspiration is what we'll explore in the next question.

Does It Inspire?

Moved People Move People

The ability to envision the future is as essential to leadership as the ability to articulate it in a way that is inspiring to others.

RICHARD SHERIDAN[1]

Malala Yousafzai was born in the Swat Valley of Mingora, Pakistan. Her father was a teacher who founded a small private school for girls in her village. He wanted Malala to have the same educational opportunities as boys her age. But when Malala turned eleven, the Taliban seized control of the Swat Valley.

In their efforts to stanch Western influences, the Taliban not only banned music and television, they also forced women into burqas and out of schools. Girls were no longer free to learn. What's more, the Taliban blew up more than a hundred girls' schools and hanged the beheaded bodies of policemen in town squares as a statement of who was in charge.[2] But encouraged by her family, Malala saw a different future for her country and the world beyond, one where access to learning was open to both boys and girls.

She went to work immediately, partnering with journalists to detail the horrors of life under the Taliban. It was risky, but she was all-in on her vision. She used her vision to motivate her country—and ultimately the world—to move the oppressed from their present woes to a future of hope. How? Not by the mere rightness of the cause. The behavior of the Taliban was immoral and indefensible, but that didn't prevent it from prevailing.

No, Malala did more than present a clear vision of a future in which every girl would be free to attend school. She courageously defied the terrorists at great personal risk and inspired the world with her vision. Even though speaking against the Taliban invited a death sentence, Malala presented a talk at a local press club, entitled "How Dare the Taliban Take Away My Basic Right to Education?"

Later that year, when the Pakistan government awarded Malala the National Peace Prize, she was asked about the risk she was taking by being so outspoken against the Taliban.[3] Standing resolutely by her vision, she said, "I think of it often and imagine the scene clearly. Even if they come to kill me, I will tell them what they are trying to do is wrong, that education is our basic right."[4]

Ten months later, acting upon orders from a notorious cleric, a masked gunman boarded her school van and demanded, "Which one of you is Malala? Speak up, otherwise I will shoot you all. She is propagating against the soldiers of Allah, the Taliban. She must be punished."[5] Upon recognizing Malala, the militant shot her, hitting her in the head and neck. It was another shot heard around the world.

Malala recovered from the attempted murder and had a decision to make. "I could live a quiet life," she said, "or I could make the most of this new life I had been given. I determined to continue my fight until every girl could go to school."[6] She redoubled her efforts to ensure that every girl around the world has access to twelve years of education. Not only has she rejected the status quo of fear and oppression, she founded the Malala Fund to foster a vision for what is possible. In the process she became the youngest recipient to be awarded the Nobel Peace Prize.

Why Inspiration Is Key

Malala's vision continues to inspire the world to change and people to invest in its realization. So moved by Malala's story, Angelina Jolie made a personal donation of $200,000 to underwrite the educational efforts of girls in Malala's hometown. In 2016, the Malala Fund attracted a $4 million grant from the Bill and Melinda Gates Foundation to "give all girls a secondary education." In 2018, Apple announced it was partnering with the Malala Fund to "educate more than 100,000 girls around the world" by providing technology and curriculum assistance.[7]

Along the way, the Malala Fund provided education for more than 1,200 children who lost the ability to attend school in Sierra Leone when the government closed schools to prevent the spread of Ebola.[8] These are the real-world results of an inspiring vision.

It's not enough to have a vision. And it's not enough for your vision to be clear. For a vision to be effective, it must

A vision that fails to inspire will surely expire.

be powerful enough to shake off complacency and replace it with the motivation to take action. Unless your Vision Script ignites hearts, minds, passion, and creativity, you won't attract the talent or the buy-in from your team necessary to reach your destination. Your customers won't buy into it either. And you'll forgo the impact and contribution that you might otherwise have on the world stage. A vision that fails to inspire will surely expire.

Does your vision inspire? There are four characteristics to ensure it does. First, it focuses on what isn't, not what is. Second, it's exponential, not incremental. Third, it's risky, not stupid. Fourth, it's focused on what, not how.

Why these four? Remember our definition of vision at the start of the book: it's an inspiring, clear, practical, and attractive picture of your organization's future, one superior to the present. If your vision of tomorrow is more or less the same as today, it fails on all points. You've got to ensure your vision goes beyond today and prompts action toward tomorrow. Let's take a deeper dive into each of these characteristics now.

1. What Isn't, Not What Is

The first gas-powered taxi was built by Gottlieb Daimler in 1897. Later that year, Friedrich Greiner started the first motorized taxi company in Stuttgart.[9] Fast-forward a hundred years or so. In 2006, more than 240 million people rode in a taxi in New York City.[10] Clearly, the taxi business wasn't a new idea. This is what I mean by the "what is."

Along came Garrett Camp and Travis Kalanick. By focusing on the "what isn't"—namely, a taxi company that didn't own any cars and didn't have any drivers on the payroll—they founded Uber. As the story goes, Garrett and Travis were unable to get a cab in Paris.[11] After their return to the States, Garrett noodled during his free time on the idea of an app-based ridesharing service. About a year later, Garrett pitched Travis on his initial thoughts. Here's how I imagine their conversation went down.

"Hey, Travis, remember that night in Paris how we couldn't get a cab?"

"How could I forget? We about froze to death!"

"Right. Here's a crazy idea," Garrett says. "What if you and I found a way to make the whole taxi process easier? Maybe we could network customers directly with their ride using an app."

Travis adds, "And people could hail a cab with the push of a few buttons. But," Travis asks, "does that mean we need to raise capital to buy a fleet of cars?"

"Actually, we won't own *any* vehicles—"

Travis cuts him off: "Seriously? Next you're gonna say we won't have any drivers."

"Good call. We won't have any drivers on our payroll either."

That's a radically transformative vision of the existing taxi model. Drivers working for themselves, with no prior taxi experience? Absurd. Drivers using a digital map for customer pickup and routing for the quickest path to the destination? That was as unheard of as was the idea that the fares, payments, and receipts would be handled through an app they'd create. Talk about constructing an implausible vision.

Today, Uber is the largest ground transportation company in the world—and they don't own their own cars.[12] Their innovative vision doesn't seem so crazy now, does it?

That's because, as Duncan Watts says, everything is obvious once you know the answer.[13] Hindsight is 20/20. Garrett and Travis could have taken the safer, more conservative road, by envisioning some sort of partnership within the existing taxi ecosystem. Or, they could have let the myriad of tactical hurdles and logistics of the "how" shut down their blue-sky ideation before they got out of the gate.

Instead, they stepped out into the future and envisioned what could be apart from the existing best practices in taxi, limo, and transit services. In just ten years, Uber has skyrocketed from a seemingly ludicrous vision of the future, to that of a worldwide company with approximately 100 million users.[14] As of this writing, Uber enjoys almost a 70 percent US market share and is valued at $72 billion.[15]

Their vision inspired millions of customers who find the new ease of transport irresistible. It also inspired legions of drivers who might otherwise have been unable to get into business for themselves, including those who just want to gain some side hours to improve their financial situation. I have my doubts that Uber would be where it is today if they had cast a tepid vision for their future, or if they had focused on "what is" instead of "what isn't."

2. Exponential, Not Incremental

You know your vision will be inspiring when you move from taking the baby steps of incremental change to pursuing giant, exponential, and pioneering ideas. Take the leap into the future when, on January 9, 2007, Steve Jobs presented the first cell phone without a keyboard or stylus. We're not talking a better keyboard; this move represented a whole new technology. He said, "iPhone is a revolutionary and magical product that is literally five years ahead of any other mobile phone."[16] He was right.

An incremental vision would have been a better physical keyboard, one with smoother action, ideally sized buttons, and so on. But Jobs recognized that one of the key limitations to the usefulness of the smartphone was the large, immovable, mechanical set of keys that took up space and limited the potential applications of the device. Imagine the apps you currently use on a screen half the size or smaller. He decided the keyboard had to go. In an exponential leap, he replaced the physical keys with virtual keys that could appear when needed, vanish when unneeded, and leave all that real estate for a bigger, better screen.

Anticipating criticism from the Nokia and BlackBerry crowd—the then leaders in the space—Jobs said, "We are all born with the ultimate pointing device—our fingers—and iPhone uses them to create the most revolutionary user interface since the mouse."[17] Even so, the skeptics were quick to weigh in. Steve Ballmer, former Microsoft CEO, said, "It doesn't appeal to business customers because it doesn't have a keyboard!"[18] I'm sure he regrets that one.

PCWorld's response was likewise dubious: "We're still iffy about the software keyboard and predictive text entry: They work reasonably well, but overall text entry is still easier with a hardware keyboard, and the iPhone may not be the best choice for people who need to compose a lot of email."[19]

Billionaire Marc Andreessen, co-creator of the Mosaic web browser, co-founder of Netscape, and a fan boy of the BlackBerry, had his doubts too. He asked Steve Jobs over lunch, "Boy, Steve, don't you think it's going to be a problem not having a physical keyboard? Are people going to be OK typing directly on the screen?" Jobs said, "They'll get used to it."[20]

Others flat out predicted iPhone's failure, including this headline: "We Predict the iPhone Will Bomb." The reviewer asserted, "That virtual keyboard will be about as useful for tapping out emails and text messages as a rotary phone."[21] These critics were wrong. Apple's exponential vision was so inspiring and attractive to customers that in July 2016, Apple celebrated selling more than one billion phones.[22] Nobody loved it but the people, all of whom would regard a physical keyboard as a massive step back now that they're accustomed to the benefits of a large screen.[23]

3. Risky, Not Stupid

Initially, all of the products we created at Michael Hyatt & Co. were digital, excluding live events. We had a membership site to help leaders build their online platform and two digital courses: one teaching our exclusive goal-achievement framework (*Five Days to Your Best Year Ever*) and another teaching our proven productivity methodology (*Free to Focus*), both of which are now also books.

We liked digital products because the costs are low, they scaled easily, and our customers could start benefiting moments after they ordered. Delivery was instant! Based on their engagement, we could tell our customers were happy. To deviate from that proven formula would be risky, but we felt we needed to.

The story of our *Full Focus Planner* serves to illustrate the point above and also works in microcosm as an example of the whole vision-creating and vision-casting process. Two things conspired to bring it about. First, we knew *Best Year*

Ever and *Free to Focus* offered not only complementary systems but essentially interrelated systems. They work better together. But we had no product that integrated them. We discussed this in our executive team meetings around the same time as several of us read David Sax's book, *The Revenge of Analog*.[24] Lightbulb! We knew it at once: we needed to create a physical paper planner, combining our goal-achievement system and productivity methodology in one simple, intuitive, portable, daily companion. The logic behind this is that if a busy executive or entrepreneur is on their phone, desktop, or tablet, they're subject to a million distractions. A physical product cuts the clutter while providing the tools to distill major goals into daily tasks.

We had all kinds of people who said, "A paper planner, are you kidding me? You are aware that this is the twenty-first century?" I fielded responses like that on social media for weeks. But our operating assumption was that if you want to get clear on your goals and your daily actions, the best place to do that was in an environment away from all the noise of, for instance, social media.

Could we fail? Sure. As a company, we had never created a planner or any other physical product before that. What if the market response was meager? What if we sunk a pile of cash in inventory we couldn't move? That's the risky part. But was it stupid? Not at all. We already knew customers loved what they were able to accomplish with *Best Year Ever* and *Free to Focus*. Combining them seemed like a no-brainer.

Beyond that, three members of our executive team—our chief marketing officer, our chief content officer, and I—all had publishing backgrounds. We knew just enough to be dangerous! A planner is more complicated than a standard trade book (like the book you're holding now), but we knew what we wanted and knew how to find the right partners to get the project off the ground.

We designed the planner and printed 10,000 copies. During the preorder phase, we sold all of them almost immediately! We actually underestimated the demand. We had to race to get a second printing done before we ran out of inventory. Every time we ordered more, we found we couldn't keep pace with the demand. We ended up selling 100,000 copies in the first year alone. We took a risk with an inspiring, transformational new product, and it paid off big.

There's a difference between a vision so big it makes you uncomfortable and one that's just plain stupid. How can you tell? Here are a few qualifying questions. Are you likely to fail? If yes, it's stupid, not risky. Does your team believe in it, or can the key stakeholders get aligned on it? If no, it's stupid, not risky. Does the risk imperil your mission? Unless your mission is already imperiled and the new vision is your plan to survive (remember the example of Fujifilm?), it's stupid, not risky.

Many businesses have made stupid gambles and survived, even thrived. But survivor bias means you shouldn't follow their lead; think of all the companies that made stupid bets, lost everything, and are no longer around to warn you about it.[25] Anything big and inspiring will be a bit risky, but it shouldn't be stupid.

4. What, Not How

Vision is about what the future looks like, not how you plan on getting there. As the smoke cleared on bombed-out girls' schools, Malala Yousafzai couldn't have mapped out a path to the Gates Foundation and donations from Apple. Nor did she need to. She only needed to make the rest of us yearn for justice, equality, and the right of girls to learn.

When I took my vision retreat after becoming publisher of Nelson Books, I knew I had to focus on my vision for the division and resist the temptation to focus on the strategy and tactics. Vision and strategy are both important. But there is a priority to them. Vision (*what*) always precedes strategy (*how*). If there's no destination, there's no path to get there. But if you have a clear vision, you will eventually find the right strategy to arrive where you want to go. Without vision, no strategy will save you.

> **Vision is about what the future looks like, not how you plan on getting there.**

I knew I needed a vision that was so big that it would inspire not only others but me as the team leader. I knew that if my vision was not compelling, I wouldn't have the motivation to stay the course once adversity came. Nor would I be able to recruit others to help me achieve my "moon shot."

Consider the reverse—that is, if I had been strategic before I was visionary. "Well," I might have said, "I don't see how we can accomplish this much. The situation is so dire. We don't have the necessary resources to do it. My team is exhausted. Let's just break even this next year. Maybe we can reduce our working capital by selling off a little obsolete inventory to improve our bottom line. Maybe we can sign a few new authors to eke out a little revenue growth."

Do you think anyone in my division would have gotten excited if I came back with that? Would that have attracted the right new agents and authors necessary to grow our list? Would it have retained the right employees? Would it have secured additional corporate resources? Would the sales team have a captivating message that would energize the retailers on our behalf? I don't think so.

By focusing on an inspiring *what*, people find their *why*. The problem with focusing first on *how* is that we stop believing in a superior tomorrow. We fail to see how we can accomplish more. We torque back our vision so it's "realistic." And because we tend to experience what we expect (Question 3), we manifest our low expectations. We grow less than we could, achieve less than we're capable of, and experience less than we deserve.

I didn't take that approach. Instead, I developed a vision I found compelling. I knew if I couldn't get excited about it, I couldn't sell it to others. I needed to give myself permission to envision the ideal future without dwelling on how we'd get there. Because thoughts of the how always strangle the what, and that means you'll never get where you really want to go.

To me, the quintessential example of what, not how, are the Wright brothers. Wilbur and Orville Wright had a vision of making a "flying machine." Many have written about their obsession (first sparked by a rubber band–powered toy helicopter), the various hazards and heartaches they faced (including humiliation and injuries), and their journey that ultimately revolutionized aviation history as we know it.

My purpose here isn't to rehearse all of those details. Instead, I just want to point out how little they focused on the tremendous obstacles they faced or the resources they lacked. Neither had finished high school or gone to college. When it came to technical training, they were self-taught. There wasn't a venture capital fund bankrolling their initiative. The competition for human flight was already intense, and many had already failed. Several people had already died. What goes up must come down—sometimes faster and harder than you want. None of that mattered, ultimately. They were so inspired by their vision of human flight, nothing was going to stop them. They were going to fly; figuring out how was secondary.

"If we all worked on the assumption that what is accepted as true is really true, there would be little hope for advance," Orville said.[26] And that's true for all of us. In almost every settled opinion, there's just enough room for error, ignorance, and insufficient analysis that someone with fresh ideas can shake up the status quo and take us from now to next. That's practically the definition of *entrepreneurialism*.[27]

Changing the Script

Would Malala Yousafzai have been successful if she told a suffering country that things could probably get marginally better? What about Uber or the iPhone: Would slightly more efficient cab service or a nicer-feeling keyboard have received the same rave response that their vision-driven leaders elicited by casting a vision for something wildly better?

"Most organizations are supremely organized around day-to-day operations," says Richard Sheridan, CEO of Menlo Innovations. That's because business as usual works like a script: we all know our lines and can deliver them like well-practiced actors. But there's usually little feeling or passion in the delivery. "Amid this practical and useful busyness, how do we move forward? How do we reimagine and reinvent ourselves?" The answer, says Sheridan, is vision.[28] To lead people beyond business as usual, we have to change the script.

The script we're most used to involves incremental gains, cost-of-living raises, the occasional promotion, and decent benefits. That script might have worked in prior years, but nowadays no one delivers those lines with any verve or passion. It's not inspiring enough. I think that's particularly true with millennials. More and more, we're motivated by creating real transformation in the world. As the vision-driven leader, it's your job to envision that transformation and enroll others to bring it about.

Your Vision Script is your tool to change the tired, discouraging story so many people are living. So, is your vision inspiring? Is there enough pull, enough passion, enough excitement baked in? As I said before, if it fails to inspire, it will surely expire. Once you've ensured that your Vision Script is inspiring, the next step is to ensure it's practical. The next question will help you further refine your vision by showing you how, at last, vision connects to strategy.

Is It Practical?

Understanding Strategy and Hiring

Achieving a goal provides immediate satisfaction;
the *process* of achieving a goal is a lasting pleasure.

EVELYN BEREZIN[1]

I'm typing these words in a word processor. It's a technology we're all familiar with. We're probably so accustomed to it, we don't give it a moment's thought. We just click the app and type. But like any technology, there was a time when it didn't exist. It took vision to imagine it and bring it to life, and Evelyn Berezin had the vision.

Raised on science fiction stories in the 1930s, Berezin graduated in 1945 from NYU with a degree in physics and did advanced work in atomic energy. Around that time, she developed an interest in computers and went to work for the Brooklyn Electronic Computer Corporation in 1951.

"The only woman in the shop, she became its lead logic designer," says Matthew Kirschenbaum, who tells her story in his book, *Track Changes*. Berezin later moved to Teleregister, where she helped develop the first computerized airline reservation system for United Airlines. Then, after being snubbed for an executive position with the New York Stock Exchange—higher-ups thought it would seem "unbecoming for a woman" at the time—she struck out on her own.

In a pre–word processing world, secretaries were employed to handle vast amounts of office paperwork, correspondence, memos, reports, and the like. The usual tool was a typewriter, and sometimes dozens of women (and they were invariably women at that time) were pooled together in a room clicking and clacking away. But as anyone who has used a typewriter knows, it's easy to make mistakes. Retype! And what about duplicating passages? You'll need to retype those too. Berezin's genius was realizing that a computer could help secretaries address these and other challenges with minimal trouble, freeing them to work more efficiently and ultimately pursue more elevated work.

It was the late 1960s, and IBM had recently created a machine called the MT/ST. It had some limited word-processing capabilities but wasn't a true computer and was less than reliable. Berezin envisioned a different kind of device, a programmable system powered by microprocessors. So in 1969 she launched her company, Redactron, and started building her word-processing computer at her own manufacturing facility. The device, which she branded the Data Secretary, started shipping two years later. She was, at the time, the only woman in the country leading a computer company.[2]

Berezin, who died in 2018, was a pioneer and a key figure in the movement that eventually led to a computer on every desk and in every home. "Without Ms. Berezin," said British writer and entrepreneur Gwyn Headley, "there would be no Bill Gates, no Steve Jobs, no internet, no word processors, no spreadsheets; nothing that remotely connects business with the 21st century."[3] Berezin herself admitted Headley overstated the case. "It would have happened no matter what," she said, downplaying her contribution.[4] But I take Berezin's story as a powerful example of how vision can inspire.

More importantly for this question, it's also a powerful example of how vision serves practical purposes, how it can inform "the *process* of achieving a goal," as Berezin put it. If you recall the leader-manager differential from Question 1, many leaders prioritize execution and view vision as secondary. But Berezin's story shows vision is essential to guide meaningful execution. She envisioned a product and a company, then she executed on that vision. The vision informed her actions. Without the vision, there would have been no product and no company.

To one extent or another, that's true for all of us. A clear and compelling vision guides our steps. And by aiming our efforts toward an inspiring future, we imbue our daily tasks with meaning and significance.

I want to address that process in this question. Is your vision practical? There are many ways to address it, but I want to focus on just two considerations: your plan and your people. For it to matter, your Vision Script must play a meaningful role when applied to the actual work of your organization, especially strategy and hiring. You'll know your Vision Script is practical if you can work to it and hire to it.

Working to Your Vision

MIT Sloan research fellow Michael Schrage sat at lunch with the leadership team of a tech-giant's R&D department. The company's new CEO had a bold vision and was redirecting organizational resources to those ends, forcing the R&D team to rethink how they were working. They asked Schrage's advice. They wanted to know how to respond. How could they keep innovation as a priority?

"I answered their obvious questions with my own," Schrage recounted. "What new innovation initiatives had they launched, and what dedicated team had they organized, to explicitly support their CEO's high-profile moves toward diversification?" The answer was . . . crickets. "With the exception of the firm's venture arm looking at a few external start-up options, no formal or informal Lab groups were directly working on their CEO's newly declared priorities."[5]

I see similar disconnects between vision and daily work all the time. When we looked at the difference vision makes (Question 2), we saw the problems created by a lack of vision: being unprepared for the future; missing key opportunities; chasing too many opportunities; making strategic missteps; wasting money, time, and talent; and quitting too soon. An impractical vision can cause the same problems. How?

The relationship between vision and strategy. Imagine you're sitting in a strategic planning meeting. You've got a Vision Script, but you don't consult it. Instead, you start with a SWOT analysis, examining your strengths, weaknesses, opportunities, and threats. The resulting analysis will be half-baked at best. Vision is a qualifier for all four categories.

Strong, weak, opportune, threatening how? In what way? To what effect? For what ends?

Unless your vision is factored into the analysis, your answers will be meaningless. But here's a corollary: unless your vision is clear enough—that is, sufficiently concrete and explicit—to help you evaluate your strengths, weaknesses, opportunities, and threats, it's not practical enough to help you plan, which means it's also meaningless. Strategy serves vision, but only a practical vision can serve strategy.

Vision is about where you're going, and strategy is the path you're planning to take. Vision comes first because there's no path without a destination. But without a path, there's no progress.

INTERPLAY OF MISSION, VISION, STRATEGY, AND VALUES

Name	Defines
Mission	who you are
Vision	where you're going
Strategy	how you're going to get there
Values	the kind of people you are along the way

Thankfully, a practical vision suggests the strategy. One of the best illustrations I know of this is the story of free-climber Tommy Caldwell. In 2008, Caldwell looked across Yosemite Valley at the three-thousand-foot rise of El Capitan. He'd already climbed El Cap about sixty times, but this time he focused on the Dawn Wall. He described it as "the biggest, steepest, blankest wall on El Capitan." Reflecting back on the moment, he said, "Its sheer improbability fascinated me."[6] Sounds like the start of an inspiring vision, doesn't it?

The Dawn Wall had been climbed once before in 1970. But the pair of climbers had to use bolts and ropes to support and hoist themselves on portions of the featureless rock face. Caldwell wouldn't have it so easy. He would use ropes, but only to catch himself in a fall. The rest of the time he would rely on his fingertips and the rubbery soles of his shoes alone.

The climb was a long process, and that process is actually highly instructive to vision-driven leaders. In 2009, Caldwell started rappelling down from the top to identify possible routes up the wall. He explained, "That's how you solve the puzzle of a big free route. You figure out a move, link a sequence of moves together, then connect these sequences until you come to a logical stopping point that marks the end of the pitch." The route up the Dawn Wall had thirty-two of these individual pitches. Soon, he said, "I had a macro-concept of the line, even if plenty of question marks remained at the crucial level of putting it together."[7]

A practical vision suggests the strategy.

The process Caldwell describes here is exactly the process vision-driven leaders employ to execute their vision. Starting with the vision and working backward, we craft a strategy, then set goals, and then break down those goals into meaningful next steps. You can climb an entire mountain like that. Keep your eye on the peak and every step counts. This is where long-term strategy and daily productivity meet.

The link between strategy and productivity. Even with clear and inspiring visions, leaders often get swamped by mundane, routine, workaday tasks and constant interruptions—not to mention occasional emergencies and crises. Writing in *Harvard Business Review*, Heike Bruch and Sumantra Ghoshal note, "Executives are under incredible pressure to perform, and they have far too much to do, even when they work 12-hour days. But the fact is, very few managers use their time as effectively as they could."[8]

Best-case scenario, this "active non-action," as they call it, involves important business-as-usual tasks for which managers and other team members are better suited. Worst case, it's low-value "fake work," to use a term coined by Brent Peterson and Gaylan Nielson.[9] Disconnected from our vision, we end up doing tasks for their own sake instead of doing so in service to something bigger and more important. Why are you writing that report, meeting with those people, working on that project, or setting that deadline? If it's not to help you realize your vision, you might be wasting time.

The truth is that there is—or at least there should be—a through line from your vision to your daily to-dos. As with Caldwell's sequence of moves and pitches, it's the sequence of next steps, goals, and strategies that takes you to the top of your mountain. I describe different aspects of this process in my two previous books, *Your Best Year Ever* and *Free to Focus*. The first covers annual planning, the second daily productivity. I want to combine them here and show how they work together. It comes down to five elements:

1. **Vision Script.** The Vision Script is the basis of everything else. As we've seen already, it's a clear, inspiring, practical, and attractive picture of your team, products, marketing, and impact three to five, though possibly more, years into the future.

2. **Annual plan.** From that vision comes this year's annual plan. What will you do this coming year to make progress on your vision? What projects will you undertake that will bring you closer? What initiatives will you

start or stop? What products will you create or retire? The clearer your Vision Script, the more apparent the answers to these questions will be. In my experience, the best annual plans identify seven to ten key goals that help leaders make progress on their visions.

3. **Quarterly goals.** If all your annual goals are due at the end of the year, you'll likely delay progress in the meantime, and you'll also overwhelm your team with activity near the deadline. Instead, you want to pace yourself throughout the year as best you can. Look at your list of annual goals. You'll want to pursue two to three per quarter. Think of these as your Quarterly Big 3—near-term objectives that can keep you focused and drive productivity, rather than promote procrastination and inevitable overwhelm.[10]

4. **Weekly objectives.** To stay on target for your Quarterly Big 3, you need a Weekly Big 3, composed of three weekly achievements that will move the needle on your major goals (as well as key projects). I recommend a Weekly Preview process in which you review your Quarterly Big 3 each week and decide what three next steps to prioritize in the coming week. It doesn't mean it's all you'll do during the week, but your Weekly Big 3 are the objectives that matter more than any others.

5. **Daily tasks.** Your weekly objectives then inform your daily to-dos. I recommend choosing just three key tasks each day—your Daily Big 3. Don't worry if that seems like too few. Trust me: they add up, and they keep you focused and on track. Once you gain the focus that comes from identifying your Daily Big 3

every day, you're going to know that no matter what else happened, you accomplished three high-leverage tasks to help you realize your goals and, ultimately, your vision.

It's worth reminding ourselves that there's a difference between our vision and business as usual, between strategic priorities and standard projects. Both are necessary, but the

ENVISION & EXECUTE

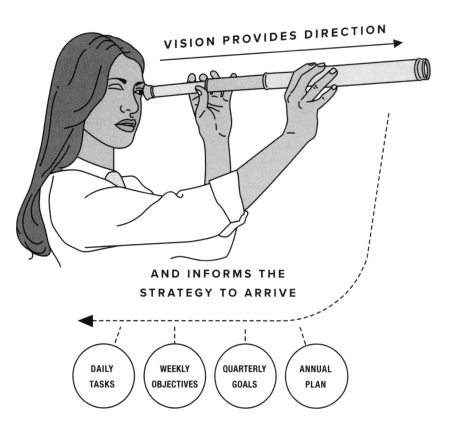

more pressing the project—the more engulfing business as usual—the less likely you are to make progress on the goals that will drive progress toward your vision. Unless you intentionally protect 40 to 60 percent of your time, as a leader, to focus on the vision, you run the risk of never reaching it.[11]

All five elements should be in alignment. Moving from the ground up, if your daily tasks don't support the weekly objectives, you won't reach your quarterly goals, which means you'll miss the annual plan and you'll then delay realizing your vision. If, on the other hand, you succeed at each step, you'll have a path all the way up the mountain, and each small step will resonate with meaning and significance. Of course, that doesn't mean it's a straight shot. It almost never is.

Many paths up the mountain. No matter how much intention and planning you employ, unforeseen problems and obstacles will emerge and force you to change your strategy. Caldwell faced this more than once on the Dawn Wall. One particular obstacle seemed impassable, but he eventually noticed a way around. "The solution escaped my notice because it's so bizarre," he said.[12] To make it work he had to loop two hundred feet out of the way to make just twelve feet of upward progress. But it worked.

And it's a key lesson when it comes to vision and its relationship to strategy. There's always more than one way to reach your destination. If you want a cake, you can (a) bake one yourself from scratch, (b) bake one from a mix, or (c) buy one from a bakery. Any of the three will produce a cake. I like to use the Waze app when driving. It crowdsources the most efficient means to get from point A to point B. But if that route becomes congested or another, more efficient route emerges, the app reroutes me. The important takeaway

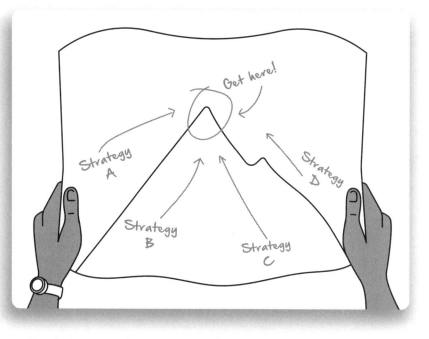

There's always more than one way to realize your vision. Vision-driven leaders recognize it's the destination, not the path, that matters.

here is that the vision is fixed, but strategies flex depending on circumstances.

Sometimes the strategies will, like Caldwell's, vary dramatically from how you began. The willingness to experiment with a diversity of strategies depends on how compelling you find the vision. Caldwell would never have gone two hundred feet out of his way if he didn't think it could help him get to the top. But because his eye was on the vision, even that unlikely route became an attractive possibility. And it proved effective.

The story of *The LEGO Movie* offers a comparable example of an out-of-the-way strategy that succeeded. After a disappointing attempt at making their own movie with total creative control—"it was boring . . . no edge," admitted LEGO CEO Jørgen Vig Knudstorp—they knew they needed a different approach.[13] Ceding creative control to the filmmakers would ensure the new movie was fun, but what if they didn't get the brand? The new movie might ding the company image and alienate fans. This was a seemingly immovable obstacle on the way up the mountain. But by staying connected to the vision, another totally novel path emerged.

What did LEGO want? To create an exciting moviegoing experience for fans while ensuring the brand was respected. So LEGO decided to give total artistic control to the filmmakers with one remarkable condition. The filmmakers had to immerse themselves in LEGO culture: spending time with LEGO's biggest fans, attending conventions, and hanging out with LEGO employees. That move, say University of Toronto professors Jennifer Riel and Roger Martin, turned outsiders into insiders without LEGO being overprotective and meddlesome in the process. It was the best of both worlds. And *The LEGO Movie* was a phenomenal success.[14]

The vision-strategy differential. The company Embrace Innovations provides another helpful example of a strategy pivot. Globally, one in ten babies is born premature. Two of my granddaughters were premies. The younger was born at just twenty-seven weeks and weighed a little more than a pound. Neonatal care in the developed world is highly advanced, but that's not the case in undeveloped countries where premies' chances are grim. In fact, about a million die each year, often because there's no reliable way to keep them warm.

THE VISION-STRATEGY DIFFERENTIAL

Vision	Strategy
What	How
Ends	Means
Destination	Path
Fixed	Flexible
Sacred	Disposable
Singular	Plural

Those figures shocked Stanford Business grad student Jane Chen, who in 2007 was tasked with her team to create an affordable solution. She accepted the challenge. "No baby should die from being cold," she said. Using some pretty advanced tech, she and her team developed the Embrace Warmer, a superportable incubator that costs about $200. Armed with her vision of saving babies and her remarkable product, she launched her company, Embrace Innovations, to make it happen.

Obstacles quickly emerged, however, especially with funding. Thankfully, Chen eventually realized there was a better way up the mountain than relying on donations and government contracts. She created a for-profit company called Little Lotus, selling swaddles, sleeping bags, and blankets based on the same tech as the Embrace Warmer. "We thought, 'What if we could leverage our technology and create a product for the US market?'" she says.

Chen built Little Lotus on the buy-one-give-one model popularized by Toms Shoes. Starting a for-profit to self-fundraise for the nonprofit was a successful steparound strategy that now helps fund the work overseas. As of 2017, according to a report in Insights by Stanford Business, Embrace Innovations "has saved more than 200,000 premature

VISION: CAKE

Strategy A:
Make from
scratch

Strategy B:
Use cake mix

Strategy C:
Buy a cake

Let's expand the cake illustration: Imagine you have a birthday to celebrate tonight and you decide to bake a cake from scratch. But when you check the pantry, you realize you're out of flour! No worries. There's a cake mix on the pantry shelf as well. The party is a few hours away when you slide the cake pan in the oven; you've got just the time you need to finish. But then the power goes out! Thankfully, you're resourceful. You still have options, including the bakery around the corner. If you were totally committed to the first or even second strategy, you wouldn't achieve your vision. Vision-driven leaders are committed to their visions and quick to change strategies as circumstances require.

babies and hopes to increase that number to 1 million."[15] The vision stayed the same, but the strategy changed.

We should expect to change strategies—sometimes many times—before reaching our destination. The Prussian field marshal Helmuth von Moltke offered this advice from the world of battle planning: "No plan of operations extends with any certainty beyond the first contact with the main hostile force," he said. "Only the layman thinks that he can see in the course of the campaign the consequent execution of an original idea with all detail thought out in advance and adhered to until the very end."

Von Moltke continued, "The commander in chief will always keep his main objective [vision] in mind and will not be swayed by the changeability of events. Nevertheless, the way in which he hopes to attain that objective [strategy] cannot be laid out in advance with any degree of certainty." Instead, he said, commanders must stay committed to their objective and use their best judgment to react as needed in the moment.[16]

We're in the same situation. No one can see three, five, or ten years down the road. We can't see one year down the road. We can't even see tomorrow, if we're honest. Remember what we said in Question 3: Vision isn't prophecy. It's a tool, not a timeline of inevitable happenings. The only way our vision will come true is by keeping it in view and working—despite inevitable obstacles and unforeseen occurrences—toward the summit. (More on that, by the way, in Question 8.)

A practical vision is specific enough to suggest strategy, but not so specific it commits you to one particular strategy. Your vision is sacred, but your strategies can switch as needed. I like how my daughter and our company's chief

We should expect to change strategies—sometimes many times—before reaching our destination.

operating officer, Megan Hyatt Miller, puts it: "The way to achieve our goals is to hold them tightly and our strategies loosely."[17]

Hiring to Your Vision

Despite having mapped the route up the Dawn Wall, Caldwell at first didn't attempt it. Why? It seemed impossible—until, that is, he met up with another climber who caught his vision.

Caldwell met Kevin Jorgeson in 2009, and Jorgeson was convinced they could pull it off. A partnership was born, and the two began training together, rehearsing moves, and building their strength and stamina. After several failed attempts—"If you do it right," Caldwell says, "failure becomes growth"—they started back up the mountain on December 27, 2014, together.[18]

Vision is a *together* kind of thing. If your dream doesn't require a team, chances are good you're dreaming too small. That's why a practical vision is good for more than planning. It's also good for people, not only in hiring them but also in keeping them aboard once you've got them.

Author Laurie Beth Jones considers vision an important recruiting tool.[19] That's true in two ways. First, a compelling vision sells the company to prospective employees. Second, it helps you filter applicants. It sets the bar and clarifies the kind of employee who best fits on your team.

Selling the company. The 2016 Gallup Report entitled *How Millennials Want to Work and Live* discovered that "only 40 percent of millennial employees surveyed felt strongly connected to their company's mission."[20] If your workforce is disconnected from your mission, if they don't find themselves energized and passionate about the vision of your company, they have little incentive to put in the extra effort, or to stay with you over the course of time.

Jim Clifton, CEO and chairman of Gallup, put it this way: "Back in the old days, Baby Boomers like me didn't necessarily need meaning in our jobs. We just wanted a paycheck—our mission and purpose were 100% our families and communities. For Millennials, compensation is important and must be fair, but it's no longer the driver."[21]

This isn't a minor point. Proportionally speaking, millennials represent the largest generation in the US labor force.[22] As of 2017, according to the Pew Research Center, millennials (ages 23–38) constitute 35 percent of the American labor force—that's more than Gen Xers (39–52) with 33 percent, baby boomers (55–73) with 25 percent, and postmillennials (18–22) with 5 percent.

What, then, is the number one driver for millennials? Finding meaning and purpose in their work. Gallup reports millennials are looking for "work that fuels their sense of purpose and makes them feel important."[23] If they're looking for meaning and purpose in their work, it's up to you to offer it.

I don't agree with Karl Marx on much, but I do value his insights on worker alienation. When people are primarily valued for their output, they become more like machines than people, and dehumanizing work environments create unfulfilling transactional relationships. A compelling Vision Script, however, has the potential to create meaning and excitement in our work. People of all sorts, not just millennials, are hungry for that and will be eager to join your organization.

Of course with an influx of applicants, you'll need a way to sort the best from the rest. Thankfully, your Vision Script can help with that as well.

Filtering potential hires. Just as vision suggests strategy, it also suggests what kind of people you need on your team. Every hiring candidate we interview goes through a series of interviews and evaluations. We're not only looking for a good fit but also to see how this person will contribute to our culture and desired results. Cultures are like chemistry. Adding and removing elements can change the dynamic. When you add, you need to ensure you don't accidentally subtract.

We keep several points from our Vision Script in mind as we consider the personality, character, work style, and skills of potential hires. For instance, the Team component of our Vision Script includes the following:

- We maintain a work culture that is fun, wildly productive, and fully supportive of our mission and values.

- Our teammates live and breathe our core ideology. They possess impeccable character, extraordinary talent, and proven track records. They are humble, confident, and enthusiastic about serving others. They are the best users of our tools, ambassadors of our message, and evangelists for our culture.

- Our employees are free to be present for their family during work hours to attend important school functions, doctor's appointments, and the like.

- Our employees experience reasonable autonomy, planning and executing their own work, without the impediment of overbearing management, stifling bureaucracy, or procedural red tape. We encourage innovation and experimentation. If something doesn't work, we learn from it and move on.

In the hiring process, these points inform the context for our conversations and evaluation. They help us craft interview questions, read the candidate, and check our impressions. The vision becomes a benchmark. Can we see this person living up to the vision for our team? Do they have what it takes to help us achieve our objectives?

There are few things more frustrating than having people you love in the wrong positions or, worse, unnecessary positions. They're frustrated and so are you. The Vision Script can help with that as well. A candidate might be a great fit for the company but not right for what the vision requires. Keeping the Vision Script in mind can prevent this problem on the front end—getting the right people pointed in the right direction from the outset. It can also provide clarity after the fact and help you make tough calls if you need to.

The filtering quality of vision is especially important when your direct reports or other department managers request new hires. It happens every budget season, doesn't it? Leaders get hiring requests that individually might make sense, but collectively would explode the headcount and undermine profitability. It's impossible (and unwise) to approve every hire. So which ones make the grade? Let your Vision Script tell you where the real needs are.

New initiatives may require new talent or they might require moving existing talent into new positions. Because the Vision Script outlines your product and marketing, it informs when and what positions to hire. If you intend to grow market share, launch a new product, start a new division, or whatever, you've got some advance thinking on timing and priorities. Your vision becomes a key factor in hiring.

Ultimately, when considering new hires you're trying to discover, first, do they embrace your vision? Second, can they help you reach your vision? It's not about who you find likable or merely having a warm body in a chair. If someone doesn't fulfill these two requirements, they don't make the cut. The last thing you can afford is hiring people that inadvertently undermine your vision.

A commitment to our vision is one way we can help ensure diversity on our teams as well. As entrepreneur Astro Teller says, "If you want to explore things you haven't explored, having people who look just like you and think just like you is not the best way."[24] In fact, Scott Page demonstrates in his book *The Diversity Bonus* that the reverse is true.

A range of dispositions, backgrounds, skills, and life experiences enhances a team's ability to solve problems. That means you'll get from point A to point B faster the more diverse your team is. Not only is wide diversity reflective of the market you serve, it's also the best way to ensure you have the smarts, skills, and sensitivities to realize your vision.

By stating your desire for a diverse team in your Vision Script, you'll be more aware of where you currently fall short. You'll also be more alert to hiring opportunities that can move your organization forward.

The Visibility Problem

After nineteen days of climbing and sleeping on the rock face suspended by ropes, Caldwell and Jorgeson made it to the top of the Dawn Wall. The right strategy and the right people came together to do something that had never before happened. But vision was the start of it all—when Caldwell saw the sun hit the Dawn Wall and decided that's the next major climb to make. From there, Caldwell's vision informed the strategy and then attracted the right partner to make the climb with him.

That's what makes a vision practical. Used properly, a clear and inspiring Vision Script becomes instrumental in its own achievement.

Unfortunately, that's where the breakdown happens for a lot of leaders today, myself included in prior years. My enthusiasm for vision meant my team and I would sometimes go on a planning retreat and cook up a huge, beautiful vision document. When we returned, it would go straight into a giant three-ring binder that fit snugly on a shelf next to all the previous versions. No one would ever look at them again. I don't think we were alone in that.

According to a Gallup survey of more than three thousand workers, only four in ten strongly agreed they knew their organization's purpose and what made it unique.[25] That's a real problem. Imagine if Caldwell and Jorgeson were halfway up the wall but clueless about what cliff they were ascending or why. If your team doesn't know your vision, they can't align their work to help you get there.

We'll go deeper on this next in Question 7, but the main point to make here is that the strategic relevance of your vision is real only if it's visible. People have to see what you, as the vision-driven leader, see. An invisible vision is pointless. As the leader, you need to embody the vision and regularly discuss it. It's your job to make sure it's in the air.

One way to ensure your people see what you see is periodic review across the company. At Michael Hyatt & Co., we do this for all our employees and their spouses at our annual retreat. We do it more often with our leadership and executive teams.

But the most effective way to keep your vision in view is to work the process already outlined in this chapter. The through line from vision to daily tasks is the most essential form of visibility because it's enacted and reinforced every day. And there's joy as tasks are checked off, objectives reached, goals accomplished, and the plan achieved, making the vision one giant step closer to realization. It's what Evelyn Berezin had in mind when she said, "The *process* of achieving a goal is a lasting pleasure."

Of course, before you get there you have to enroll your team and others in your vision. The acid test on any vision is whether you can sell it. This includes selling up, down, across, inside, and outside your organization. We'll explore that challenge in the next question.

Can You Sell It?

Enrolling Your Team

Selling a dream means transforming a vision—that is, an insight that is not yet perceptible to most people—into a cause and getting people to share that cause.

GUY KAWASAKI[1]

During the nineteenth century, Montgomery Ward was the world's largest retailer. Quite a feat considering they had no retail stores. As a mail-order company, Montgomery Ward sold their merchandise exclusively through massive catalogs, the internet of their day. Then, in 1886, a railroad agent who sold watches as a hobby launched his own mail-order business. His name? Richard Sears. Within a few short years, thanks to lower prices, Sears's catalog business surpassed Montgomery Ward.

To keep pace, Montgomery Ward hired Robert E. Wood in 1919 to be their general merchandise manager. Wood had excelled in a similar role while working as the number two man on the construction of the Panama Canal. They hoped he could boost Montgomery Ward's profitability and compete with Sears's pricing. He was successful at that job. But Wood was more than a manager. He was a vision-driven leader.

Wood looked to the future, and with the Model T Ford fueling the automobile revolution, coupled with the Federal Highway Act of 1921, he sensed that significant changes in consumer buying habits were on the horizon. The population shift from rural to urban living offered further evidence to support this assessment. In 1920, for the first time ever, more Americans chose urban over rural living, a move that transformed the retail industry.[2]

In 1922, convinced that the newfound mobility would ultimately kill the mail-order business, Wood envisioned a future where retail stores would serve the majority of their customers. Wood presented this vision to Montgomery Ward's president, Theodore Merseles. He lobbied Merseles to move away from catalog sales to a retail store model. Merseles refused. For two years, Wood made it his personal mission to get Merseles to consider at least test retailing, but Merseles wasn't buying.

Wood did find a buyer for his vision, however. Sears hired him and tested the store idea. Wood opened the first test store on February 2, 1925, just three months after joining the company. They opened seven additional stores before the end of Wood's first year. Spurred on by his success at Sears, Montgomery Ward finally got the picture and entered the field in 1926.

The Sears retail-store concept caught on like wildfire, and in less than a decade, with Wood now promoted to president, Sears opened 374 stores nationwide. Quite an accomplishment given they were making the business up as they went along. When he started, no one in the company knew the first thing about running retail stores. Thirty years after Wood came to Sears, revenues had soared from $200 million to almost $3 billion.[3]

The surest test of your vision is whether you can sell it to four key stakeholders: your immediate team, the organizational leadership (if you're the CEO, this might include your board or investors), to the rest of the company down the chain, and across the organization. Depending on how your company is wired, you may also choose to sell your vision outside of the company to watchers in the media.

As Wood discovered, vision-driven leaders are engaged in a bit of a dance. We have scripted a crystal clear vision of our future reality, one large enough to inspire others, one that also stirs up enough uncertainty to make us take a deep breath like we're stepping into a swimming pool filled with cool water, and yet we have to sell it to the team with full confidence. And they have to buy.

"You will find it necessary to leave what is comfortable and familiar in order to embrace that which is uncomfortable and unfamiliar," as Andy Stanley says. "And all the while, you will be haunted by the fear that this thing you are investing so much of yourself in may not work out at all."[4] Sound fun? That's just part of the drill when creating and selling a compelling vision.

But it's an essential part of the process. No selling, no progress. So can you sell your Vision Script? Now that you've conceived the dream, it's time to think through enrolling others. We'll look at this critical task across several different relationships: first, your direct team; second, your boss (or your board); third, the company more broadly; and fourth, outside the company if necessary.

Selling Inside

Let's say you've written your Vision Script. You've ensured it's clear, inspiring, and practical. But at this stage, as I've mentioned, you're not descending Sinai with the tablets. Your vision is still a first draft, capable of reshaping and improvement.

And that's a plus. Invite refinement from key stakeholders. Not only will you get vital input to improve your vision, people more willingly support what they shape. "The best vision," as former CEO and consultant Dan Ciampa says, "will come from a disciplined, iterative approach that enables the leader to control how the picture is crafted, while also ensuring that others who need to be aligned feel some ownership."[5]

I find it's best to start with your direct reports. You want to be collaborative here, not dictatorial. "I've spent some time reflecting on how to improve our future destination," you might begin. "This is not about what I'm going to accomplish. Rather, here's what I believe we could collectively do with all of the talent in this room. I need and welcome your input." You want their input and validation, yes, but more importantly, you want to enroll them in a journey that you're going to take together.

I like to think of this internal discussion as tackling three interrelated challenges: change, personnel, and feedback.

1. The change challenge. Most Vision Scripts require changes in how you will do business, which some team members will embrace and others will resist. Some love change. They're always up for an adventure. They enjoy variety and aren't fearful of shaking the snow globe. They're quick to see the need for, and benefits of, change in order to get the win.

Others place a high value on predictability and certainty. They don't rock the boat and are usually unnerved when others rock their boat. They're happy or at least satisfied with the status quo and could feel threatened by the implications of your vision. Like leaders and managers, both types of employees are necessary. You need people who can run the ship while others make changes. The goal with selling is gaining alignment, not changing people. You've got enough change to manage without adding that to the mix.

I like to start with those who don't like change. The goal is to make them feel validated by helping them understand there's an important role for them continuing to do certain aspects of what they've been doing. So, when you roll out your vision, it's important to say, "Here's what's *not* going to change." In those very words. Your vision should be clear, and so should the language around your vision. As Beau Lotto said, you need to speak "in black and white."[6] This gives certainty-seekers on your team something to hold on to during the changes you're proposing.

2. The personnel challenge. Job description and job security play a part when discussing a new vision. Your immediate team wants to know: Is my job going to change? Is my compensation going to change? Is my title going to change? If you can legitimately say this, assure them, "We envision a place for each of you in this new plan for the future." It's useful to explain exactly what will change and what will stay the same. But we also have to be realistic.

The person they need to be in the future may require them to stretch and grow because the company is in a different place. When I shared my Nelson Books Vision Script with my team, I framed it this way: "We certainly want to create a future for you, but you have to decide if you want to be part of that future by growing." If you say something along these lines, the implication is that if you don't want to grow with the vision, we're going to get somebody who does. That's how committed we are.

Leaders hang on to people too long in my experience. We build relationships with our team, and it's hard to acknowledge the forks in the road. This challenge becomes tougher without a vision. And the opposite is also true: the clearer you are about your vision, the easier it is to spot who will help and who will hinder your progress. A Vision Script is more than a filter for hiring (Question 6); it's also a filter for retention. Your job as the vision-driven leader is to help your team either grow in their job or find one better suited for their talent and temperament.

> **The clearer you are about your vision, the easier it is to spot who will help and who will hinder your progress.**

You've probably heard that everybody is tuned in to the radio station WII-FM: What's In It For Me? *If I'm going to take this journey with you,* they're thinking, *what does that mean for me? What's my upside?* They want to know why this new vision will be good for them and why they should care. Making more money for the company isn't a winning motivation by itself. Nor is helping you succeed. Why should they care?

Here's how I approached it at Thomas Nelson. I noticed we hadn't received a bonus in several years. Part of my vision was that everybody would earn their bonus. I also noticed that everyone in my division was exhausted and overworked. So, I explained that if we're the top-performing division in our company because we added bestselling authors to our roster, and if we cut our list in half, their lives would be easier. Framed another way, "With this new vision, you'll get to love your work again." Best of all, they would have the potential to make more money via our bonus program.

3. The feedback challenge. One of the biggest reasons leaders fail to welcome constructive input is that we're not in the right headspace to do it. We're moving too fast. We're in that turbocharged, efficiency-driven mindset. We come into a meeting and it becomes all about making decisions or getting a desired outcome. Get in, get out, and go to the next one. Don't make that mistake!

Slow down. Feedback is too important to skip or rush. The team reveal can help you test and improve your vision. Remember, you're meeting with humans who have unique perspectives, backgrounds, knowledge, and problem-solving approaches. They see things differently than you do, and you need that. That's why you hired them! When you ask for their feedback, you have to stop, step back, and distance yourself emotionally so you can hear their answers. Why? Sometimes you're not going to like what you hear.

Don't be defensive. "Be quick to listen, slow to speak," as James said a couple of millennia ago.[7] If you're not careful, you'll jump back in to sell them harder, and that will shut everybody else down. You'll leave the room mistakenly thinking you have the team's buy-in when in reality you will have missed a key opportunity to fine-tune the proposal and win their support. As Andy Stanley has said, "Leaders who refuse to listen will eventually be surrounded by people who have nothing significant to say."[8] You don't want that.

Selling Up

This will mean different things depending on your starting place. If you're a division leader, selling up the chain may include your vice president or the executive team. If you're the president, selling up the chain would be your board of directors.

As Wood discovered at Montgomery Ward, sometimes the Keepers of the Status Quo may resist your vision in outward and underhanded ways regardless of your starting point. These tactics include the slow death by a thousand spreadsheets, requests for recalculations, focus-group testing, multiple pitches, and business cases. Sometimes you get stuck with a boss who just can't or won't pull the trigger on a project, ever.

I once worked for a man like that. I would bring him a request with all the supporting documentation. He would ask me to rerun it. When I came back, he would want it rerun again, and again. It was an endless doom loop. I could never get him off the dime. By the time he approved it, the opportunity was lost, and he would blame me for missing it. It was utterly dispiriting.

One thing all bosses have in common is the dislike of surprise. Whether you're dealing with a difficult boss or an exceptional one, the last thing you want to do is to catch them off guard. Your immediate supervisor needs to hear your vision directly from you, not from somebody they meet in the hallway. Nor do you want them to discover your vision for the first time in the presence of everybody else, especially the people they're trying to lead. If you embarrass your boss or catch them flat-footed, you lose.

When selling up, timing is everything. Since you invested several days crafting your Vision Script and talking about it with your team, you don't want to be rushed when you bring it to your boss. You'll also want to schedule a time when your boss is likely to be the most receptive. You know your boss or board. Don't walk into a quagmire you could have easily avoided by being more intentional upfront.

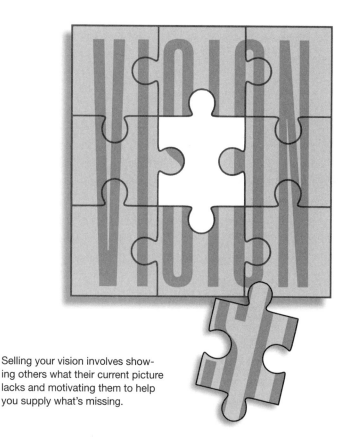

Selling your vision involves showing others what their current picture lacks and motivating them to help you supply what's missing.

What about the pitch itself? Here are five steps I have successfully used over my forty-plus years in business. I'm discussing them here in the context of selling up the chain, but they have implications for selling across and even outside your organizations.

1. Commit to success. When I had a boss, I had a basic rule: Don't take a swing unless I'm confident I'll hit the ball. The goal here wasn't to avoid risk, but to make sure I was fully committed before I stepped up to the plate. I would encourage you to do the same. Don't make the pitch unless you intend to make the sale. Your credibility is at stake—with your boss, your peers, and your direct reports.

I used to work for a guy who couldn't sell his boss (eventually my boss) anything. This was unfortunate for me, because my proposals often exceeded his approval limit. He would then have to take my proposal to his boss for sign-off. In the beginning, he enthusiastically approved my proposals and promised to get his boss's approval. However, almost always, he would come back with his tail between his legs, mumbling about how unreasonable his boss was.

Eventually, he started procrastinating going to his boss. He knew he would get rebuffed and didn't want to appear powerless to me. As a result, my proposals would languish on his desk, waiting for an approval that would never come. After about six months of this behavior, his boss sensed my frustration. He then asked me to start reporting directly to him.

Frankly, based on my previous boss's comments, I dreaded the prospect of reporting to the big boss. I assumed he was an unreasonable, capricious tyrant. However, I found him to be exactly the opposite. He was a great listener and sincerely wanted to help me. He made quick decisions and never impeded my progress. I worked for him for three years. My ability to get quick decisions from him enhanced my credibility, both with him and my direct reports. They knew they could count on me to get the approvals they needed to accomplish their goals—and mine—in a timely manner. My ineffectual boss never did that, to his loss.

Choose your battles and prepare thoroughly.

The key here is to choose your battles and prepare thoroughly. Eventually, you will develop a reputation for getting things done. This reputation will actually make it possible to pre-sell your boss before you ever say one word. They'll be thinking, *If Sally is recommending this, it is worth serious consideration. I can be confident she has thought it through and asked the tough questions.*

2. Understand the customer. The first and most important key to getting to yes is to focus on your boss's or board's needs, not yours. They listen to the same radio station as the rest of us, and the song they hear has just two verses:

- Achieve their own vision and goals for the organization
- Do so while improving profitability and other success metrics

If they can hum along with your vision, you've got their ear. If not, you're likely dead before you start. So before you schedule a time to pitch your proposal, answer the question, How is my Vision Script going to help my boss achieve their goals? If you can't answer that question, you're not ready to make the pitch.

For example, when I was a COO, one of my vice presidents wanted to add two graphic designers to his publishing unit. With salary, benefits, and other overhead, this was going to cost about $100,000 a year. However, rather than lead with this, he said, "Boss, great news. I figured out a way to save the company $100,000 a year." For me, that translated into additional profit, so I was immediately interested.

He then explained how we were already spending about $200,000 a year in outsourcing cover designs for a particular category of books. He convinced me that we could cut our expenses in half by bringing this function in-house. He made it a no-brainer because he showed me how his proposal met my needs.

3. Think through your presentation. In my experience, the number one reason people don't get to yes with their boss is because they haven't done their homework. They simply haven't thought through what and how to present their "ask." As a result, their approach is full of holes. Each of these provides an easy out for the boss—and a quick no for you.

To avoid a rejection and secure your approval, you need to rehearse your presentation and cover all your bases in the right order. First, start with the conclusion. It is much easier for your boss to concentrate if they know what you want upfront. This keeps them from wondering where you're going with your presentation.

Second, provide the background. Be brief. Provide only the background necessary for them to make an intelligent decision. A paragraph is sufficient. Stay focused and keep moving.

Third, provide the rationale. List three to five key reasons why your boss should accept your recommendation. This should include both why they should approve it as well as the consequences of not approving it.

Fourth, establish a timetable. Indicate when you will implement the proposal if approved. If the rollout will be done in segments or phases, briefly outline the key milestones. Underpromise and overdeliver on your expected delivery dates.

Fifth, state the financial impact. State this both as the cost or necessary investment and the return on investment. Be clear. Shoot straight. Don't downplay the costs or hype the benefits.

4. Anticipate objections. This is where the battle is won or lost. Unfortunately, it's a step that most people skip to their own detriment. Spending thirty minutes working on this aspect of your proposal is the best investment you could make in securing a sign-off. Think of every question or objection your boss could possibly ask. Your work in Step 3 will make this easy.

Don't risk getting a no because you haven't carefully thought through the questions and possible objections. Play devil's advocate. List the likely questions and objections, and then answers for each. Don't go crazy. A few points should be sufficient for each objection. I used to type this up on a separate document that I took to the meeting with my boss. I kept it in my folder for reference.

5. Make the pitch. Now you're finally ready to sell. First and foremost, maintain eye contact. Any documents you place in front of the boss or board are intended to be a "talking points" list rather than a narrative. You should be familiar enough with your Vision Script by now that you can stay focused and read the room.

This is Selling 101, but stay alert to the signals. Does your boss appear bored? Pick up the pace. Do they have a question? Stop talking and let them ask. Hint: If your boss engages you in a discussion, this is a good thing! It means they're interested. Are they distracted? Let them get refocused or reschedule the appointment. The last thing you want to do is plow ahead, oblivious to the reactions of the very person you're trying to persuade.

When you get to the end of your presentation, restate your recommendation and ask for a decision. This isn't purely informational. Ask for the yes you want. Then, and this is critical, shut up. Give your boss a chance to say yes. This may make you feel uncomfortable, but, trust me, you will decrease your chances of success if you pitch longer than necessary. Sometimes, your boss just needs to sit there and absorb your pitch. Resist the temptation to fill the vacuum with words.

A related point: Know when you are done. If your boss approves your recommendation, say thank you and that's all. I can't tell you how many times I've seen a person in authority give their approval and then watch the presenter proceed to *unsell the sale*. So when the boss says yes, thank them for their decision to pursue your vision, collect your belongings, and leave the room. If you can't leave, at least change the subject. Don't reopen a successfully closed chapter.

Selling Across

When selling your vision to peers and colleagues in the organization, do so privately and in advance of selling it down the chain. Actively listen and talk through any questions or concerns they may have. This gives you a golden opportunity to gauge their reaction and satisfy any apprehension they may have. You may also at this point gain insights that will help you sell it down the chain—and even further refine the vision.

Begin by creating a list of influential stakeholders, determine who you will contact first, and then quietly make visits or calls before the wider rollout. This includes divisional or department leaders, anyone with supervisory responsibility. Be sure to give your key leaders time to process the change you're calling for, provide input, and work toward alignment.

You may not always be able to get agreement, but you can get alignment. Individuals may disagree with the direction you are taking. But if they feel they have been heard and considered, they will generally align with the decision and support it when you call for that. Alignment means that no one publicly second-guesses the decision or the process as you roll it out. If a new concern develops, they bring it back to you or the group to consider.

Selling Down

Leaders encounter a lot of problems, but poor company-wide communication is one problem they often create for themselves. In fact, according to one Harris Poll, nine in ten employees say it sabotages the success of executives.[9] The same study found the second biggest problem area for leaders was a lack of clear direction. I think this probably applies across the board—in everything from casting a vision and reinforcing the mission and core values, down to day-to-day operations.

I get it. Sometimes, as leaders, we think we've said what needs to be said. We're actually worried about overcommunicating. We don't want to sound like a broken record. Back at Thomas Nelson, when talking about our vision at the company-wide level, I felt like I repeated myself a lot. I began to fear that I was wearing people out by repeating the same things over and over.

I expressed my concern to a consultant. But she said no. "When you get tired of hearing yourself and you think that everyone is starting to get annoyed," she said, "you're about half done." It was an important insight. What's crystal clear for us is often fuzzy for others. Our job is to bring definition through repetition. The truth is, you can't overcommunicate your vision to the organization. It's impossible.

People can't read your mind. We all know this. But most of us forget. When we force people to guess what we're after, we widen the margin for error and misunderstanding. You need to get what's in your mind into the minds of your teammates. That comes only with communication.

People forget and drift off course. No matter how clear your strategy and tactics are to you, others will forget. The Distraction Economy in which we work exacerbates this problem. As leaders, we can do things to combat that, and we should. But we also compensate by continually communicating what's important to our teams. Andy Stanley sometimes says it this way: vision leaks. People in your organization will lose sight of the vision you communicated days, weeks, or months ago. No one retains it all. Constant communication helps people hold on to what matters most.

Finally, some people probably haven't bought the vision to begin with. Just because people work for you doesn't mean they agree with the direction you want to take the organization. If you're serious about results, you'll either need to bring those people up to speed or let them go.

Communication around the vision is a critical factor in team alignment around your Vision Script. And team alignment is a critical factor in hitting organizational goals. Since vision leakage is a reality, the only thing keeping your vision alive is your words. Just as you have to continually water a plant so that it can grow and thrive, you, as a leader, will sustain the growth and vitality of your organization by repeating the vision over and over again.

Selling Outside

When I first joined Thomas Nelson, communications with most of our staff were not where they needed to be. There was a joke at the time that was all too accurate. If you worked at our publishing house and wanted to know what was coming next, you'd just have to find out about it by reading the *Tennessean.*

Candidly, our CEO did not get along with the business-page reporter, who broke story after story before our CEO informed his own employees. When I took over the company, I took a different approach. I invited that reporter out to lunch and established a working relationship with him. It was a good step, but that was only one small part of what I changed.

I realized that the reason the company was so prone to leaks was that instead of an information flow, what we had created was a vacuum, punctuated only by unexpected changes. We couldn't fix the problem by plugging leaks or freezing out reporters. What we really needed was a whole new communication strategy. This was especially true where large changes were involved. Any major change was met with leaks and shock and backlash. It seemed to me there was a way to avoid all of that.

There were five steps we needed to do well when pushing any new initiatives if we wanted to make real progress as a

Just as you have to continually water a plant so that it can **grow** and **thrive**, you, as a leader, will **sustain the growth** and vitality of your organization by **repeating** the vision over and over again.

company. These five steps are still applicable today for any leader pushing through a major organizational change.

First, *figure out what you want to say.* Get crystal clear on your message. Articulate what you're doing, why you're doing it, and the implications for your company and your customers.

Second, *once you've decided on the message, write it down.* I always start by writing a press release. You'll also need talking points to prepare you for speaking publicly about the change. Think headlines, sound bites, and simple, clear statements. Also start an FAQ and refresh it as questions come in.

Third, *contact influential external stakeholders.* Selected VIPs outside the organization are well worth personally contacting. This may include significant investors if you're a private company, key customers, vendors, authors, agents, collaborators, donors, and so on. For obvious reasons, you will want to make those connections prior to going public. You can do this before, during, or after you update your team of the change, but it should be within a couple of hours at the most.

Fourth, *announce the change through the press and social media.* Send out a press release and use social media. If you've done your job, this will not be news to those who care about this the most. They will have already heard from you or your colleagues personally. It's also a good idea to actively monitor social media responses so that you know what people are saying about your changes. Don't be afraid to jump into the middle of a conversation and respectfully correct the narrative if needed.

Fifth, *make yourself available to answer questions.* Generally speaking, it's a bad idea to hide from the media. My office responds to every media inquiry. We do our best to answer every question, even if we have to admit that we don't have the answer—or can't comment.

In my experience, the media are almost always respectful if they feel respected. That means being responsive and being honest and perhaps developing a relationship with key reporters and influencers. Remember, if you have a relationship with people, they're more likely to give you the benefit of the doubt if the communication gets muddled, as it might in spite of your best efforts.

Respect the Past

One final thought before leaving this topic of selling the team on the dream. I got some excellent advice when I stepped into the role of CEO at Thomas Nelson: "Always respect the past because anything that's currently in place was established as a solution to a worse problem." The existing vision, mission, and strategy may be flawed, but you don't know what they replaced, and what exists may be a lot better than what they had before you arrived.

Some leaders, impressed by the verve and daring of their vision, despise the past. These kinds of leaders are often free with their opinion, regardless of whom they humiliate or ridicule. It's better to say, "What we've been doing up to this point has worked. I'm just wondering if there's another solution out there where we can take it a step further—just like you did the last time when you brought in this solution."

One of the challenges with trying to introduce change without giving people that context with the past is that it robs them of an opportunity to evaluate. If they can see how they won the last time there was a change, they can think,

Oh, I can see us doing that again. This helps mitigate their fear of a new change in direction, and nobody feels as if they must defend the past because you're not putting it down. You're doing the opposite. You're esteeming the past.

And with that you're also setting the table for a robust consideration of the future based upon the fact that you're living in a different time, with different market conditions, new technologies and tools at your disposal, and more historical data to draw upon as you seek to accomplish a refined vision of the future. So, can you sell your vision?

A vision-driven leader will gain the support of their team when they lead with respect and humility. And effective leadership sells their vision by appealing to both the noble and daily interest of key stakeholders.

Now, in spite of your best efforts to respect the past and sell your teams, you are guaranteed to face resistance, because as I've discovered, resistance is part of realizing any vision. The vision-driven leader accepts that fact as part of the journey on their way toward their desired future. But they don't just have to roll over in the face of roadblocks, disappointments, miscalculations, or other barriers. You can have a plan in place to push through the obstacles you encounter. I'll walk you through those steps in the next question.

PART 3

THE CHALLENGE AHEAD

Impossible is just a big word thrown around by small men who find it easier to live in the world they've been given than to explore the power they have to change it.

AIMEE LEHTO

The plan is the generator. . . . So much the worse for those who lack imagination!

LE CORBUSIER

The best ideas aren't instantly embraced. Even the ice cream sundae and the stoplight took years to catch on. That's because the best ideas require significant change. They fly in the face of the status quo, and inertia is a powerful force.

SETH GODIN

How Should You Face Resistance?

Dealing with Obstacles

Everyone has a plan until they get punched in the face.

MIKE TYSON[1]

On January 27, 1967, the eyes of the world watched as three Americans took their seats inside the most sophisticated spacecraft on earth: the Apollo 1 Command Module. Designed as a preflight training exercise for the first manned lunar launch the following month, a successful dress rehearsal was vital to maintain the tight schedule. Team NASA knew the stakes were high. The clock was ticking.

The pressure was on to fulfill President Kennedy's vision of "landing a man on the moon and returning him safely to the earth" before the end of the decade. JFK's challenge was as bold as it was fraught with danger. The astronauts needed to travel a quarter of a million miles in eight days, make a pinpoint landing on the unknown substrate of the moon, initiate a launch back into space, navigate a return to Earth, and reenter our atmosphere—without burning up.

The Apollo 1 mission pushed the existing limits of what was then known about space travel. Prior to this audacious moon shot, the US had made only one successful manned space flight, a fifteen-minute suborbital trip. While the Mercury Space Capsule demonstrated that man could function while traveling at a speed of almost Mach 7, its peak altitude was a mere 116 miles; the spacecraft never left Earth's outer atmosphere.[2]

From that modest beginning, NASA scientists and engineers had to partner with more than 20,000 outside vendors and universities for additional technological support. After all, their computing power was incredibly crude by today's standards. "The software that controls what happens when you move your mouse on your PC . . . takes more memory than all the NASA supercomputers put together had for Apollo," one programmer reflected.[3] Or put it this way: your smartphone has more computing power and memory than what NASA had to put a man into space. According to one report, the "limitations of the technology were so numerous and the calculations so complex that the best that the engineers could hope for was getting as close to certainty as possible."[4]

When faced with technological and design setbacks, roadblocks, and resistance, the words of JFK echoed in the halls of NASA: "We choose to go to the moon in this decade ... not because [it is] easy, but because [it is] hard, because that goal will serve to organize and measure the best of our energies and skills, because that challenge is one that we are willing to accept, one we are unwilling to postpone, and one which we intend to win."[5]

Kennedy offered the country a clear, inspiring, and practical vision. And we signed up. But despite years of careful calculations, meticulous troubleshooting, technological breakthroughs, endless computer renderings, months of simulator practices, and the combined efforts of more than 300,000 NASA employees and contractors, Apollo 1's preflight exercise ended in disaster.

After entering the spacecraft, astronauts Gus Grissom, Ed White, and Roger Chaffee sealed the hatch. While running through a checklist, an electrical spark ignited the oxygen-rich cabin air and engulfed the cockpit with flames. Within sixty seconds, all three astronauts died of asphyxiation.

The fatal fire almost put an end to the space program. The subsequent investigation into the tragedy by NASA and Congress put the space program on hold for the better part of a year.

There are few constants in life, but resistance is one. There are no friction-free visions. The best face hardships, miscalculations, setbacks, disappointments, and other barriers to success. The question is, How do you, as a vision-driven leader, respond? How should you face resistance?

Before I share three essential traits to respond effectively, I want to explore the nature of the resistance itself and look at several examples. Some resistance is environmental, some is social, and some is psychological.

Conditions on the Ground

Environmental resistance is often the most obvious to see, and it's easy to understand. As Menlo Innovations CEO Richard Sheridan points out, organizations are optimized for business as usual.[6] Trying something new creates automatic inefficiencies. Redeploying talent, shifting workloads, and managing shoestring budget allocations (or none at all) are only the start of the challenges.

Ideally, we want to work on tasks where we are our most passionate and most proficient. If you've read my book *Free to Focus*, you know that's the Desire Zone, and it's where we typically make our most valuable contributions to our organizations. But all bets are off when we try to get new initiatives off the ground. Leaders regularly take on tasks at which they are neither passionate nor proficient because they're sometimes the only people on the team able or free to get the project started. For instance, launching the *Full Focus Planner* required members of our executive team to negotiate with printers, fulfillment centers, and even handle some of the design. Was it efficient? No. But it was effective. Could we have staffed for it? Maybe. But it was better to test the idea before hiring, and that required the executive team to get involved at a granular level, at least for a while.

Beyond similar organizational and structural challenges, environmental resistance also takes the form of economic and technological limitations:

- When President Kennedy spelled out his vision for the moon, NASA had more logistical barriers than solutions. NASA lacked the computing power to make complex mathematical calculations (one telling scene in Tom Hanks's *Apollo 13* is when NASA engineers whip out their slide rules to solve the unfolding crisis in space). They didn't know the condition of the lunar surface for purposes of landing and astronaut mobility. Nor did they know how their craft would handle in lunar conditions.[7]

- When Evelyn Berezin conceived of programming her word processor, Data Secretary, no one had done that before (Question 6). She knew she could handle the programming. But there were few sources for the microprocessors to run her program. She thought she had the right vendor—a little startup called Intel. Unfortunately, it turned out they weren't equipped to make the chips she needed. So Berezin had to change course and find another vendor.[8]

- Tim Cook became CEO of Apple in August 2011. Instead of having free rein to build his own vision for the organization, he was forced into crisis management just six months into the job. Footage revealed troubling work conditions at Apple's biggest manufacturer in China, and low-paid workers rioted. Cook hired an independent auditor who recommended 360 "remedial action items" regarding conditions, pay, and safety.[9] Important fixes, but not what he planned on doing right out of the gate.

- Garrett Camp and Travis Kalanick's vision to link drivers with riders (Uber) required industrial-strength software programming and an app that didn't exist. But, arguably, their larger challenge was creating the appropriate "mental positioning" within the mind of the rider. Hailing a cab using an app was a foreign idea; potential customers had no idea how the experience worked. A popular meme on social media summed it up:

> 1998: Don't get in a car with strangers.
>
> 2008: Don't meet people from the internet alone.
>
> 2019: Uber: Order yourself a stranger from the internet to get into a car with alone.

- Sony launched its ebook reader in 2006. Noting its high-tech specs and sleek shape, one observer compared it to the Lamborghini of e-readers. But a great product isn't everything. Sony depended on publishers to sort out contract issues with authors whose deals were crafted in pre-digital days. Meanwhile publishers were antsy about the safety of their intellectual property on Sony's platform. While Sony struggled to resolve these issues, Amazon moved into the market with the Kindle, solved the same issues better and faster, leveraged their vast book-buying audience, and upstaged their competitor with a superior user experience.[10]

There are endless manifestations of environmental resistance like this. Entrepreneurs run out of money. They experience production delays. Costs balloon. Marketing campaigns flop. They can't get a product to work as promised. Again, as Alan Kay said, "the best way to predict the future is to invent it," but invention is bumpy. Some leaders overcome environmental resistance, and their visions thrive. Others cannot, and their visions die, as happened with the Sony Reader.

But such resistance is also predictable, even if the specific problems remain hidden until they arise. It's the same with social and psychological resistance. The difficulties differ, but these challenges are also predictable.

No, We Won't Wash Our Hands

Dr. Ignaz Semmelweis, a Hungarian obstetrician, arrived at the acclaimed Vienna General Hospital in 1846. He became alarmed by the mortality rate of maternity patients. Nearly a third of his patients died from "puerperal fever," also known as childbed fever.[11] It wasn't just in Vienna. During the eighteenth and nineteenth centuries, childbed fever caused half a million deaths in England and Wales.[12]

Semmelweis was determined to find the underlying reason for the disease. He started by observing that women served by midwives survived at a much higher rate than did those served by doctors. He then noted the doctors started their day "performing barehanded autopsies on the women who had died the day before of childbed fever. They then proceeded to the wards to examine the laboring women about to deliver their babies."[13]

What! Didn't they know about germs? Not yet, they didn't. Semmelweis concluded that cadaver particles transferred to the healthy mothers resulted in their deadly contamination and instituted a radical innovation: hand-washing. He insisted that his physicians wash their hands in a chlorinated lime solution "until the smell of the putrid bodies they dissected in the autopsy suite was no longer detectable."[14] The results were both immediate and dramatic, lowering the death rate in the physician-run ward to below that of the midwife ward.

Instead of praising the life-saving breakthrough, Semmelweis's superior, Johann Klein, actively opposed hand-washing.[15] But Semmelweis was undeterred. On May 15, 1850, he addressed a gathering of fellow physicians to share his hypothesis and personal findings. Like Klein, his audience was outraged by his theory and ridiculed his insistence on hand-washing.

Semmelweis attacked his critics with a vengeance, at times denouncing them as "irresponsible murderers." But the more pugnacious he became, the more "the savior of mothers" ostracized himself from the medical community. Tragically, he was literally run out of town. A plot was hatched and executed to have him committed to an insane asylum, where he was beaten by guards and died two weeks later.[16]

On his deathbed, the forty-seven-year-old doctor reflected upon his yet-to-be realized dream: "When I look back upon the past, I can only dispel the sadness which falls upon me by gazing into that happy future when [childbed fever] will be banished."[17] That happy day came years after his death. Today, he's hailed as both a genius and the "father of infection control."[18] But his vision was rejected in his own day.

The Semmelweis Reflex: Outside and In

Semmelweis's story has given us the term "Semmelweis reflex" or the "Semmelweis effect" to describe the common phenomenon of opposing a new vision or understanding because it upsets too many apple carts. Unlike the environmental factors we saw before, this brand of resistance is social. The doctors who rejected Semmelweis's view, for instance, could not accept the idea that their healing hands were dealing death, and they weren't about to listen to his recommendations.

Vision-driven leaders regularly deal with some version of the Semmelweis reflex. The more daring the vision, the more pronounced the reflex. The reflex could happen in public, such as when Apple announced the iPhone in 2007 or when it announced the Apple Watch in 2014. Early response to both products was polarizing.[19]

But the reflex can also happen within an organization. In some organizations it's constant, and the leader either wearies of the fight and leaves or is shown the door. "Organizations say they want progress," say authors Bill Jerome and Curtis Powell, "but they really don't want to change."[20]

Vision-driven leaders bring energy, innovation, and growth, but they also question the status quo and challenge key assumptions. That can create instability and uncertainty for change-averse colleagues and bosses. This is why change agents aren't always appreciated. As Jerome and Powell observe, "Their passion is not always welcomed, understood, or long suffered. In return for their persistence for improvement, they are rewarded with labels such as 'disruptive,' 'uncooperative,' 'intolerant,' and 'insensitive.'"[21]

Whether outside or inside an organization, this version of the reflex is external. But there's another, more pernicious version—when the reflex is in our own mind. That's the psychological manifestation of resistance. And this one is also predictable. As you prepare yourself to share your Vision Script with your organization, expect internal resistance to your vision.

We can be our own worst enemies when it comes to this. How? By allowing doubtful thinking, anxiety over the outcome, or the fear of rejection to keep us from selling our vision with confidence. You may wonder, *Is this vision too radical for my team to embrace?* Or, *Is the vision grand enough to inspire participation?* Or, *What about those who resist the necessary changes?* Or, *Will we flame out while implementing the vision?* Or, *How will we ever find the resources to pull this off?* In the midst of those questions we can experience our own reflex and shut down the vision.

I understand. Most any honest leader will too. This topic comes up whenever I coach business owners and executives. If I ask how many people in the room feel they're out over their skis—that it's just a matter of time before someone finds out they don't know what they're doing—and ask for a show of hands, it's remarkable. Three quarters of the room admit the feeling. When you work and play at the edge of your abilities, it's easy to feel that. At the same time, working and playing at the edge of one's abilities is exactly why most of the people with their hands raised are also successful leaders.

So, what if we didn't allow all those doubts and limiting beliefs to have the last word? Since your vision is the snapshot of a new, brighter future, isn't it worth overcoming the stumbling blocks that our internal resistance and fear throw in our path? We, as vision-driven leaders, can leverage our inner strength to lead with courage and confidence in spite of the resistance.

Whether it's an external or internal reflex, the key thing is to stay connected to your why. I've been teaching this tactic for years now because it's basic to any vision. When you hit the wall, when you feel the resistance, the answer is to remember what's on the other side of the wall and why it matters to you. If it's launching a new business, saving an existing business, bringing a new product to market, whatever, we have to stay plugged into that vision like it's our personal power generator.

When you hit the wall, when you feel the **resistance**, the answer is to remember what's on the **other side** of the wall and why **it matters** to you.

It's also important to keep negative emotions at arm's length. When resistance rears its ugly head, it's not the facts of the situation that are the problem, but how we respond emotionally. While we need to stay emotionally connected to our why, we can't let negative emotions swamp us. We may experience fear, doubt, and disappointment, but we don't have to let them dictate our actions. We can notice them for what they are, refuse to let them control us, and keep moving forward.

Three Traits That Beat the Resistance

I've identified three essential traits you can leverage when the resistance threatens to thwart your vision: tenacity in the face of rejection, integrity when tested by ethical compromise, and courage in the face of settling for less than success.

1. Tenacity. With the exception of boxers, nobody gets punched in the face as much as creatives—for instance, artists, authors, songwriters, and painters. Having been on both sides of the desk, I can say rejection is part of the creative process. Rather than abandon their efforts, successful creatives keep showing up to work. They exhibit extraordinary perseverance when struck by the inevitable blows of rejection. Let's walk a few steps in their sneakers. Their experiences can be instructive for vision-driven leaders who will, likewise, endure outright resistance to the future they envision and present.

Creatives begin with a vision for what could be. They imagine stories, songs, and graphic art possessing the power to captivate our imaginations, move us emotionally, even motivate social and political action. They see a reality that doesn't exist—yet. And they will go to great lengths, making significant personal sacrifices, to give life to those ideas.

After days or months spent facing self-doubt, usually working in isolation, they emerge hoping their creation finds an audience. If it's a song, they play their tune for song pluggers or a music publisher in hopes that they'll pitch their music to a recording artist who, in turn, will hopefully put it on their next record. If it's a book, they'll email a book proposal and sample chapters (in some cases, a completed manuscript) to literary agents for representation and/or directly to publishing houses. If it's a painting, they may seek a gallery in hopes of having it placed on display. And then they wait. They pace. Some pray.

Regardless of the outcome, creatives create. They press on. Even though, more often than not, their dreams are met with bad news. Sometimes there's a faint ray of hope from an initial level of interest, but for a hundred reasons, things don't pan out. "Sorry, loved your song but it didn't make the final album cut." Or, "Your book, while intriguing to me, didn't resonate with the publishing board." Or, "There's no room in the gallery after all."

When Herman Melville submitted his manuscript with an unconventional antagonist he was rejected out-of-hand by the publisher Bentley & Son. They referred unkindly to the "somewhat vision-impairing length of the manuscript" and, gutting the heart of the story, said, "First, we must ask, does it have to be a whale? While this is a rather delightful, if somewhat esoteric, plot device, we recommend an antagonist with a more popular visage among the younger readers."

Discard the whale in *Moby Dick*? For what? Brace yourself. "For instance," they said, "could not the Captain be struggling with a depravity towards young, perhaps voluptuous, maidens? We are sure that your most genial friend and fine author, Nathaniel Hawthorne, would be instructive in this matter? Mr. Hawthorne has much experience introducing a delicate bosom heaving with burning secrets into popular literature."[22] Seriously.

Virtually every noteworthy creative has experienced the demoralizing blow of rejection. Like being punched in the face, they can wobble back upright and go another round. Or, they can throw in the towel. Melville's tenacity prevailed. He pursued the editors at Bentley until they finally published *Moby Dick*, sans voluptuous maidens.

"If nobody offers [a book deal] within three years," Mark Twain once said, "the candidate may look upon this as the sign that sawing wood is what he was intended for."[23] I'm glad John Grisham didn't pay attention. After penning his first novel, *A Time to Kill*, he submitted sample chapters and a query letter to several dozen publishers and literary agents, sixty in total.

His mailbox overflowed with rejections, forty in all. Imagine what that constant flurry of rejections must have felt like. Nobody would give him the time of day. And then, a nibble. He landed a small deal, and the publisher printed five thousand copies. Today, with more than 300 million units in print, I'm confident Grisham is glad he never traded his vision for sawing wood.[24] "I never thought of quitting," said Grisham. "My attitude was: 'What the heck, let's have some fun.' Honestly, I believe I would've sent it to several hundred people before I would have even thought of giving up."[25]

I'm nowhere near the same league as Grisham or Melville, but I've got my own rejection story to add. I spent the better part of a year painfully crafting my first book, shoehorning my writing into late nights and weekends. When the time finally came to solicit a publisher, I emerged from my writing cave feeling triumphant. In that moment, I had a fresh appreciation for the words inscribed on a monastery wall: "The book is finished. Let the writer play."[26] I shipped off the manuscript with great expectation, feeling like a kid on Christmas morning ready to open presents.

But no. My "firstborn" book was handily rejected by one publishing house after another. Their letters declining my work were like someone saying my baby is ugly. I pressed on. Over the course of several months, more than thirty publishers responded with a big fat no. Right up until one finally said yes.

You know what? Not long after publication, I got a call from my publisher telling me that my book had hit the *New York Times* list! Now *that* was beyond incredible. Best of all, in spite of the initial mountain of rejections from publishers who didn't buy into my vision, it stayed on the *New York Times* list for twenty-eight weeks.

> **What might the world lose if you don't see your vision through the inevitable obstacles and rejection that you're bound to encounter?**

None of that would have happened if I hadn't stayed the course with a firm grasp on the vision I had for my book. Without tenacity and the ironclad commitment to what I envisioned, I might have thrown in the towel. Who could have blamed me, right? The "professionals" had spoken. First ten, then twenty, then thirty publishers, like judges at a talent show, gave me the gong and sent me packing.

As a vision-driven leader, you can probably relate. Fortunately, tenacity can fortify you as you work through the resistance. As the authors cited above can attest, the payoff is worth the pain. What might the world lose if you don't see your vision through the inevitable obstacles and rejection that you're bound to encounter?

2. Integrity. Shortly after I rolled out my vision for turning around Nelson Books, I got some news that threatened to stop us dead in the water. We were off to a good start, but then a friend flagged me down and mentioned one of our biggest authors was advocating views divergent from mainstream, traditional Christianity. It might seem like inside baseball to some of you, but since Thomas Nelson is a Christian publishing house, this was a big deal.

Initially, I dismissed it. But over the next few days, I heard similar reports from others. I finally visited the author's website to confirm the facts for myself. Some of what I read didn't pass the sniff test. But, refusing to jump to conclusions, I enlisted the help of two theologians I respected to make sure I wasn't misunderstanding anything. Nope. They corroborated my worst fears. "This is a very serious problem," they both assured me.

This wouldn't have been so bad, except we had paid an enormous sum of money for the author's next book. We had just sent the final designed pages of her manuscript to the printer and expected it to be our biggest book of the year. Frankly, given our division's financial condition, we needed the book to succeed in a big way. I was counting on this new release to give us the lift we needed.

I decided to discuss the issue with the author directly. I supposed her errors were unintentional. After all, it's not as if she was a trained theologian. I hoped to bring her around to my stance. But she didn't budge. Over the course of a two-hour meeting, she preached at me nonstop, indignant I had challenged her and adamant everyone else—including virtually every Christian since the First Ecumenical Council in AD 325—was wrong on this topic.

Fortunately, my boss came to the meeting. He heard every word himself. We had a problem. If we published the book, we would be in conflict with the vast majority of the Christian market. Worse, it would violate our corporate integrity and my own conscience. On the other hand, if we didn't publish the book, we would lose the anticipated revenue, which was huge. We would also take an enormous write-off from the royalty advance we had paid but would not recover.

When we got back to the office, my boss asked me for my recommendation. I told him I thought we should stop the presses (literally) and cancel the book. Knowing the implications of that, he pushed back. "But there's nothing in the book itself that is objectionable," he said. "Why can't we just print her book and not publish anything more from her in the future."

"I wish it were that easy," I said. "The problem is that she is teaching this stuff publicly. If we publish the book, we are aligning ourselves with her and indirectly promoting her message." He shook his head in disagreement and told me to think about it overnight.

I went home and told Gail that I thought my career as the publisher of Nelson Books—a job I had held for less than six weeks—was already over. I was discouraged and, frankly, disillusioned. This was not what I had envisioned. Gail was supportive. "You can't violate your conscience," she told me. "Trust God, do what is right, and I will support you—regardless of the consequences."

The next morning, I again met with my boss. "Look," I said, "I am not trying to grandstand here, but I can't publish this book. Trust me, I understand the financial consequences—and I truly hate the thought of the negative financial impact this will have on us. But we'll just have to take our lumps. If you insist on publishing the book, I'll have to resign. It's a matter of conscience." My integrity was on the line.

He didn't take that well. He dismissed me from his office with a wave of his hand. He told me he'd think about it and get back to me. I went back to my office, convinced I'd be unemployed by the end of the week at the latest. Mentally, I was already packing my office.

Then, about thirty minutes later my phone rang. It was Sam Moore, the CEO of Thomas Nelson. He was on the road and had just gotten off the phone with my boss, who reported directly to him. "Mike," he said, getting straight to the point as he usually did, "tell me your side of the story."

I explained what had happened, including my recommendation to cancel the book. He asked how much that would cost. Wincing, I gave him the exact number. "Mike," he said, without hesitating for a moment, "I agree with you. Cancel the book. It's the right thing to do."

I was stunned but relieved. We hit some other obstacles as the year progressed, of course. But I'm convinced that one was, in fact, the opportunity that tested our integrity as a company and our commitment to the vision of our division. God sometimes places obstacles in our path as leaders. Why? Not to destroy us but to develop us. And without personal integrity, we risk violating the trust of our teams, our peers, our clients, and our customers in pursuit of our vision.

As a postscript, we not only achieved our budget that year, we surpassed it. How will you respond when your integrity is tested? Zig Ziglar put it this way: "It is true that integrity

alone won't make you a leader, but without integrity, you will
never be one."[27]

3. Courage. People get energized with new visions. The
creative spigot runs hot. Ideas flow. The team is alive with
possibility. But then the next stage of work begins. A few
people report on the assignments they were given. Maybe
they share a sketch, a proposal, or a demo. It's not bad; it
might even be pretty good. But it doesn't quite meet with
expectations. Something is missing.

Everyone is polite. A few even make suggestions. But some-
where deep inside, you realize that the dream has taken a
hit. It hasn't died, of course. But it has been dialed back—
calibrated to the reality of deadlines, budgets, and limited
resources. The *how* encroaches on the *what*. At this very
moment, you face a decision. Will you take a stand for the
original vision or will you—and everyone else in the room
following you, the leader—concede? The one thing that will
keep this from happening is courage.

Courage gives life to the vision once the initial enthusiasm
wears off. In my experience, there are several ways to find
the courage you need to swim against the tide and defend
your vision. It starts with taking a stand for greatness. Like
many important things in life, creating and selling a vision
begins with making a commitment. You must resolve in your
own heart that you will not settle or sell out. When you
decide that the dream warrants it, you have to take a stand
and play full-out.

Next, you need to connect with the original vision. Before
it exists, it's only an idea. No matter how clear and inspiring
your Vision Script, the only place your vision exists in all its
brilliance and color is inside your head. Sometimes, you just

have to close your eyes and once again become present to what you are trying to create in your future reality.

Now, remind yourself what is at stake. I have found that the best way to do this is to ask, "Why is this so important?" When I was writing my first book, I had a list of seven reasons why I needed to write the book. I reviewed it every morning before I began writing. It gave the project an almost epic significance, but it kept me going when I wanted to quit.

It's important at this point to listen to your heart. Most of us have spent a lifetime ignoring—or even suppressing—our intuition. I don't know if this is a product of modern rationalism or American pragmatism. Regardless, I believe intuition is the map to buried treasure. It is not infallible, but neither is our reason. And, it can point us in the right direction. We need to pay attention to this inner voice.

Now you're ready to speak up. This is the crucial step. You must give voice to your heart and go on the record. If you don't, who will? You may be the last chance of the original dream to stay alive. Most people will give in, give up, and move on, especially if they feel the pressure of how over what. Most people have more to do than they can get done, so they are reluctant to go through one more iteration to get it right when there's a workable compromise in sight. But if they don't, they will never experience the awesome fruit of your vision. This is why you can't afford to remain silent. As the vision-driven leader, you must advocate for the vision.

Finally, be stubborn. This is perhaps the toughest part of all. We all want to be liked. We don't want to be high-maintenance or unreasonable. But think back on your own history. Aren't the people you respect the most also the ones who demanded the most from you? You may not have fully appreciated it at the time, but, looking back, their stubborn refusal to settle is what made the difference.

Notice I didn't say be a jerk about it. There's a difference between being stubborn and being rude. One way to leverage that difference is humility. The most effective leaders are often those who exhibit humility at critical moments. Why? It goes a long way toward shouldering the load, as well as sharing the failures and wins with the team.

When we lead with humility, we become approachable, likeable, and inspiring. And trust me, there are days when the team gets hit hard with a curveball. Humility in those moments keeps the team unified. Meanwhile, pride divides and demoralizes.

> **Since resistance is predictable, we have to ready ourselves for its appearance. That means not only cultivating our tenacity but also holding on to our integrity, and expressing courage.**

Since resistance is predictable, we have to ready ourselves for its appearance. That means not only cultivating our tenacity but also holding on to our integrity, and expressing courage. If vision is something our teams expect from us (Question 2), this is one of the times they need it most. Don't let them down. There's no reward for giving up. On the contrary, history provides us example after example of persistence in the face of resistance and the rewards that followed as a result.

Resistance and Rewards

The Apollo 1 disaster was a devastating blow to Kennedy's vision of superiority in space. But it contained a silver lining.

•

The accident galvanized NASA to redouble its commitment to execute their mission by fine-tuning their processes, protocols, and procedures. Because they pushed through the setbacks that threatened to derail them, Kennedy's vision became a reality on July 24, 1969, when Neil Armstrong splashed down in the Pacific after walking on the moon just days before.

Examples abound. The vision for the first Chrysler minivan was rejected by virtually every internal stakeholder because it didn't fall into an existing car class and their competition didn't have anything similar. Incoming CEO Lee Iacocca saw the potential, yet the "bean counters initially tried to block it."[28] The innovation not only saved Chrysler from bottoming out, it revolutionized the automotive industry.[29]

Steve Jobs had a vision for Apple's Macintosh computer but got thrown out of the company he founded. Against all expectation, Jobs then returned to Apple, saving the company from bankruptcy and reinventing it with his vision for the iPhone. Apple became the first "American public company to cross $1 trillion in value."[30]

And then there's Dr. Semmelweis. He suffered for his vision of hand-washing to stop the spread of infectious disease. Years after his death, his pioneering vision triumphed, leading to countless lives being saved and paving the way for Louis Pasteur's germ theory of disease.

Business as usual produces predictable results. But if you want something fresh, something new, that takes vision. Greatness only happens by design. And, while the vision-driven leader is committed to designing and pursuing a desirable future outcome for their organization, they recognize resistance is part of realizing their vision. To become the most effective vision-driven leader, tenacity, integrity, and courage are essential.

Do you have it in you? I believe you do. But perhaps you're thinking about how vision lines up with the current reality of your organization. You're wondering if it's too late. That's the question we'll take up next. The good news is that at any stage of an organization's growth curve, vision plays a part and can even revitalize zombie companies.

Is It Too Late?

The Power of the Vision Zag

Many of life's failures are people who did not realize
how close they were to success when they gave up.

THOMAS EDISON[1]

We are on a burning platform," the vice president reported to the board. "We're running out of cash . . . [and] likely won't survive." News nobody wants to hear, but when Jørgen Vig Knudstorp broke it to the LEGO leadership in 2003, he was speaking the truth.[2] It might be hard to remember today, in a time when LEGO is recognized as one of the world's most successful brands, but at the turn of the millennium it almost went bust.[3]

Company revenues had been on a steep incline since the 1970s, but profitability dropped in the nineties, largely from competition. Not only did the company's patents expire, inviting new players on the field, but the traditional toy market also struggled against growing demand for video games and electronic educational toys. What's more, kids had less time for unstructured play because their schedules were increasingly jammed with weekend sports and after-school activities. It's hard to assemble large, complicated sets when you're drilling at soccer practice.

Desperate for a hit product to overcome its market erosion, LEGO tripled the number of new toys it produced between 1994 and 1998, hoping for a breakout success. Then following the advice of outside consultants and turnaround specialists, it expanded into clothes and jewelry. It partnered with new licensees. It opened theme parks. It built a video game division from the ground up.

Revenues surged, but costs surged more. The majority of efforts either masked what was wrong or made matters worse, since management didn't have systems in place to determine what was working and what wasn't. Instead of regaining its foothold, LEGO lost its way and almost went bankrupt in the process.

When revenues collapsed in 2003—prompting Knudstorp's warning—the company was neck-deep in debt with a business so sprawling and complex it couldn't manage its own inventory. LEGO was falling to pieces. Thankfully, the leadership soon realized Knudstorp was right, promoted him to CEO, and reinvented itself under his leadership.

When we ask, *Is it too late?* the temptation for some is to look at our circumstances and jump to yes. But are they right? Countless businesses fail every year at all stages of life—Startup, Legacy, it doesn't matter. Yet companies with one foot through death's door, such as LEGO, stage comebacks more often than you'd guess. They do this through something I call the Vision Zag. Think of it as re-visioning.

In companies that Zag, vision-driven leaders come up with new and inspiring directions for their organizations. Any company can accelerate with the right Zag, and any company can avoid decline—even completely reinvent itself—with one too. Remember the story of Fujifilm told in Question 2. And here's the thing: organizations can perform this move at any life stage. We'll look at several of these companies below using the Vision Arc. This will allow you to see where and when they Zagged, and where you might Zag as well.

THE VISION ARC

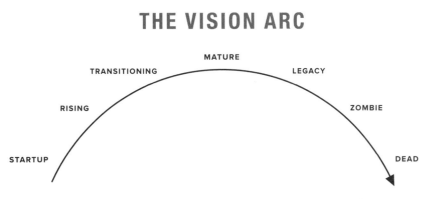

The Vision Arc depicts a standard business trajectory through time with decline in profitability as a seeming inevitability. But is decline inevitable?

The Vision Arc

As I see it, there are seven stages of a business: Startup, Rising, Transitioning, Mature, Legacy, Zombie, and Dead. These are not rigid categories—more like convenient points on a continuum. I call it the Vision Arc, and I find it helpful to plot businesses along the curve based on their stage. Depending on the organization and how much history it has, you can follow it from birth to the grave. Now and then, companies pull a Lazarus and Zag back to life. But even companies in the early and middle stages Zag when they need to.

The Vision Arc offers a picture of profitability over time. Profitability increases as a startup successfully navigates from inception to maturity, where it faces either decline or renewed viability through a Vision Zag. A Zag occurs when an organization effectively jumps back to an earlier stage on the Arc, a maneuver we'll follow below by examining several companies who managed the maneuver.

Note that the profit and time are not absolute; they're relative to each company, and every company is different. Note also that not every business goes through each stage. Some can fail in the Legacy stage, as LEGO nearly did. Some fail to survive the Transitioning stage, as my indie publishing venture did. And some never make it past the Startup stage.

The Vision Arc is relevant since, as author and business analyst Steve Denning notes, "Half a century ago, the life expectancy of a firm in the Fortune 500 was around 75 years. Now it's less than 15 years and declining even further."[4] Denning goes on to ask the right question: "What would happen if [a] firm opted to keep playing offense and focus totally on adding value for customers?" Knudstorp did that with LEGO, and the results speak for themselves. LEGO is now one of the most successful companies in the world.

The Vision Zag occurs when a business defines a new vision and, in turn, experiences a fresh round of investment, energy, and market growth—even if the company is a Zombie or Dead. Why does this matter? Without an effective vision, you're stuck wherever you are. You might languish in the land of a Startup or Rising company where you can't seem to get to the next level, or you might be a stagnant

Legacy company on the verge of heading to obsolescence and death.

Regardless of your current position on the Vision Arc, your company can deploy the Vision Zag to extend its vitality and profitability. As you'll see, it's never too late to get started with a revised vision. Nor, I should add, is it too early. Some companies have to Zag right from the gate, when their initial vision fails them.

The Startup Zag

During the Startup stage, the dream is king. It's a time of wonderment and discovery. Your passion runs high for the new endeavor, but without a vision you're sure to flounder eventually for all the reasons we've already covered (see, especially, Question 2). Complicating matters is a steep learning curve fraught with too many unknowns that all new businesses face. For example, Where will you find customers, how will you connect to them, will they want your product or service, and what is the threshold to become a viable business?

The temptation during a Startup is to rely mainly on hunches and intuition for direction. What's really needed is carving out the time to define your vision. That's ultimately what brought the curtain down on my indie publishing venture. We didn't have a vision to help us filter which books to publish. Nor did we have a vision to guide our scaling efforts.

But even Startups with a vision often find themselves in trouble when their initial vision doesn't pan out as hoped. The ones that survive are the ones that Zag. "Research has shown . . . that the vast majority of successful new business ventures abandoned their original business strategies when they began implementing their initial plans and learned what would and would not work in the market," says Harvard Business School professor Clayton Christensen.[5] Indeed, that's what we see in the next two case studies.

Airbnb's Zag. The original vision for Airbnb wasn't a global empire built upon a network of privately owned accommodations. Rather, it emerged when cofounders Brian Chesky and Joe Gebbia needed to make some extra cash to cover their rent. In 2007, while living in San Francisco, they caught wind of the fact that there wasn't enough hotel capacity to handle a major conference. They quickly bought several airbeds and offered a place to stay—and breakfast—for $80. It worked. In 2008, they applied that approach during the Democratic National Convention in Denver when the demand for temporary housing eclipsed the supply. Again, a modest success, but not enough to build a real business on.

That's when the partners realized their vision was too small. A Vision Zag was needed that, at first, appeared laughable: creating a worldwide network of local hosts renting out spare rooms to travelers as an alternative to traditional hotels. "Everyone thought it was crazy," says Chesky. "No one supported us. We had no money. It was the best weight loss program ever—I probably lost twenty pounds because I didn't have any money for food."[6]

Although Chesky believed he was onto something, his new vision was crazy enough to frighten him. He described the early days like one long, continuous Groundhog Day, waking up filled with a chest-pounding panic, followed by some level of confidence that things would work out, then waking up the next day in a panic again.

Part of his panic was a byproduct of the string of rejections from financial backers. Their concept of hospitality services initially attracted zero interest from investors who, Chesky recalls, would literally walk out halfway through the presentation. "Most people thought it was insane."[7]

It took several years and three different website designs before their radically transformative idea resonated with both the public and a number of venture capitalists. But it did, and today, Airbnb is in 34,000 cities and is the world's largest accommodation provider. Unlike Marriott, Hyatt, Hilton, or any of the other global players, they own no property and enjoy a valuation of about $35 billion.[8] All because their original vision wasn't big enough. And so they Zagged.

YouTube's Zag. Cofounders Steve Chen, Jawed Karim, and Chad Hurley first envisioned a video-dating website. In 2005, they launched YouTube with the sole purpose of connecting potential sweethearts. "We even had a slogan for it: Tune in, Hook up," said Karim.[9] To attract users, the partners took out ads on Craigslist in several cities, offering to pay women $20 if they'd upload a video describing their dream date. They got the cold shoulder. When nobody took them up on their offer, Karim wasn't entirely surprised. "We didn't even know how to describe our new product," he said, an extreme version of a very common problem for Startups.[10]

And that's when the founders Zagged. "Okay," Chen said, "forget the dating aspect, let's just open it up to any video."[11] To kick off their new vision, Karim posted "Me at the Zoo," an eighteen-second clip of him describing elephants. He said that's when users "began using YouTube to share videos of all kinds. Their dogs, vacations, anything. We found this very interesting." The lightbulb moment followed: "We said, 'Why not let the users define what YouTube is all about?' By June, we had completely revamped the website, making it more open and general. It worked."[12]

In 2006, Google acquired YouTube for $1.65 billion.

The Rising Zag

On the upslope of the Vision Arc, the ride is thrilling. The team is excited. It's all blue skies. But vision-deficit leaders often run into trouble at this stage. With no vision to guide their strategy and decisions, as we saw in Question 2, they often chase the wrong opportunities, miss the right ones, and pay the price. A clear vision at this stage can point leaders to the right opportunities for growth. What if they don't have a

THE VISION ZAG

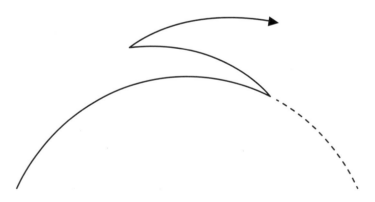

The Vision Zag allows you to re-energize your organization by re-envisioning your future. To use Microsoft CEO Satya Nadella's phrase, it's how to "hit refresh" in your business. Compared to the Vision Arc (p. 185), this diagram shows a Zag at the Legacy stage, but leaders can Zag whenever necessary.

vision or their vision is outdated? Just like Startups, Rising companies can course correct with a Vision Zag, yielding astonishing results.

Instagram's Zag. In 2010, Kevin Systrom originally created an iPhone app called Burbn, named for his favorite adult beverage. Conceived as a competitor to Facebook, Foursquare, and Gowalla (now defunct), Burbn allowed users to check in at locations for meetups, earn points for hanging out, and post pictures of their time together.[13] Systrom figured he could outdo the competition. And, true, he had something, but it wasn't working the way he wanted. His early adopters provided initial success, but the app was widely viewed as too cluttered and difficult to navigate.

In his book, *Blue Ocean Strategy*, author W. Chan Kim says it's a mistake going head-to-head with the competition, as Systrom initially did. "Blue ocean strategy challenges companies to break out of the red ocean of bloody competition by creating uncontested market space that makes the competition irrelevant," he says.[14] Ultimately, that's what Systrom did. After teaming up with Mike Krieger, the duo discovered their users weren't using the check-in feature at all. They didn't care about earning points either. Rather, Burbn users loved taking and posting pictures. And that was enough for a new direction.

Systrom and Krieger chopped out all functionality from Burbn except the ability to take, comment on, "like," and post photos. On October 6, 2010, they launched the overhauled app, renaming Burbn as Instagram. Within twenty-four hours, twenty-five thousand users had downloaded the app. Three months later, more than one million users were sharing and liking photos on Instagram. On April 12, 2012,

Facebook bought Instagram for $1 billion. Today, Instagram is worth more than $100 billion.[15]

Starbucks' Zag. As the story goes, "Over lunch and a bad cup of coffee," Gordon Bowker, Jerry Baldwin, and Zev Siegl decided to redefine what a cup of coffee should taste like.[16] On March 30, 1971, the trio rented a Seattle storefront from which to sell bulk coffee beans along with the gear to grind them. A decade and four stores later, sales hit $4.4 million. While the company sold beans and high-end grinding machines, Starbucks didn't sell actual cups of coffee at first—just the means by which customers could make them at home. That was the extent of their vision.

Howard Schultz joined this Rising boutique firm in 1982 as director of operations and marketing for Starbucks. A year later, Schultz attended an international housewares show in Milan, Italy. While there, he fell in love with the espresso bars, lattes, and the way the bars served as community gathering places. "This is the perfect drink," he thought after the first sip. "No one in America knows about this. I've got to take it back with me."[17] But when he proposed a Vision Zag to the three owners—that they change their business model from equipment and product vendors to cafés—they threw cold water on the idea.

Schultz, in turn, left Starbucks to open his own coffee firm, Il Giornale Coffee Company, reflecting his experience in Milan. In spite of the fact that nobody could pronounce the name of his store (Eel Joe-rrnah-leh), it was a hit. He quickly opened two more locations. About a year later, Schultz's three Seattle stores "were on track to make $1.5 million a year."[18] His tremendous growth allowed him to buy out and acquire his bean supplier—his old employer, Starbucks—

which was then strapped for cash and overextended. In 1987, he rebranded his coffee shops as Starbucks and brewed his way into more than 30,000 locations worldwide and $24 billion in sales as of this writing.[19]

The Transitioning Zag

In the Transitioning stage, companies are like the shrubs in the front yard in late spring. They've grown, but they've grown all over the place. This is usually a time to prune in preparation for the next big move. It's a natural stage at which to validate and revise your original vision. Which assumptions remain true, which have proved false?

At this point it's tempting to stick with the original vision—and all the unruly growth it inspired. But now's the time to make smart choices about the future, especially when it comes to the products you offer and the customers you serve. This is true of companies, divisions within a company, and brands.

JVC's Zag. During the 1970s, JVC and Sony battled for supremacy to become the industry standard with their respective videotape recorders. Sony's technologically superior Betamax system offered better video and sound quality with less noise, and its cassettes offered one hour of recording time. At first, Sony had the upper hand, controlling 100 percent of the home video market simply because it was first to market.

Meanwhile, electronics company JVC saw an opportunity to outmaneuver, rather than parrot, what Sony had created. Primarily known for televisions and radio consoles, JVC began experimenting with videotape. They Zagged and introduced their lower-cost VHS format. While the picture quality was not as good as Beta, VHS provided two hours' worth of tape. Sony lost the market. It was enamored with the quality of its creation and failed to recognize that consumers cared more about runtime than picture quality; Beta cassettes couldn't even hold an entire movie![20]

How did Sony miss something so obvious? They assumed customers wanted to record only their favorite TV shows, in which case a one-hour tape worked fine. And, having sold 100,000 units in the first year, they felt validated in their assumptions.[21] They didn't account for the fact those sales were made *before* VHS hit the market. Once customers discovered the lower cost and longer runtime of VHS, as well as the ability to record or play back full-length movies, they gravitated to VHS's cheaper format.

Sony tried to Zag at that point, but the video-rental business market had emerged by then and it was too late. "By the time it had become clear that home movie viewing, not taping TV shows, would be the killer app of the VCR," writes author Duncan Watts, "it was too late [for Sony]."[22] Within the first year, the VHS format captured 40 percent of the market share from Sony. By the late 1980s, nine in ten VCRs sold in the US were VHS.[23]

Netflix's Zag. When Netflix decided to do a Vision Zag in 2007, from mailing DVDs in little red envelopes to becoming primarily a streaming platform, they were met with outright skepticism. Time Warner CEO Jeffrey Bewkes questioned the sustainability of a business model built around streaming movies. "It's hard to see how that kind of economics can fit into a service that charges $8 or $10 a month because the math doesn't work," he said.[24]

And, then there's that unforgettable moment when Netflix's cofounder Reed Hastings pitched Blockbuster's CEO, John Antioco, the vision of running Blockbuster's brand online while Blockbuster ran Netflix's brand in their stores. Antioco and his team couldn't see it. "They just about laughed us out of their office," recalled Barry McCarthy, Netflix's then CFO. "At least initially, they thought we were a very small niche business. Gradually over time, as we grew our market, [Antioco's] thinking evolved, but initially they ignored us and that was much to our advantage."[25]

Meanwhile, Netflix's transitioning from a DVD subscription model to a streaming model was rooted in their ability to "adapt to changing technologies and consumer demands," and "this ability to adjust has continued in recent years with the success of the company's original content."[26] As a result, Netflix was ranked as the highest-rated TV network among US consumers as of April 2018,[27] while their original content earned twenty-three Primetime Emmy awards in 2018.[28] And, their annual revenues spiked from $997 million in 2006 to more than $16.61 billion on March 31, 2019.[29]

Meanwhile, as of this writing in 2019, there is just one Blockbuster store left open in the entire world. It's in Bend, Oregon, if you want to try picking up a copy of *The Breakfast Club*.[30]

The Mature Zag

Companies in the Mature stage have survived the turbulence of the Transitioning period. If this is you, you're well established within your industry. Your customers are loyal and readily embrace and depend upon your products or services. You face competition from other mature companies, which places a downward pressure on pricing. You've reached the peak of the revenue and earnings ratio, which has largely stabilized.

Anticipation of significant future growth is not expected because it's likely you're approaching market saturation in your target demographic. This is when optimization of resources and scaling through acquisitions allows you to appease investors who still desire growth in earnings. But there's still opportunity to innovate, acquire, or expand through a merger. Unfortunately, this is also the stage at which companies that lack vision become complacent and lose control of the ship. That was the state of affairs when Steve Jobs returned to Apple.

Apple's Zag. Jobs returned to Apple in 1997 at a time when sales had tanked 36 percent in just two years—from $11 billion in 1995 to $7 billion in 1997.[31] Revenues from their biggest moneymaker, the Mac, were sagging, and Apple was three months away from running out of money.[32] Without a significant Zag, Apple was through.

The first thing Jobs had to do was keep the company solvent. He struck a deal with Bill Gates: Apple would drop a tired and costly lawsuit against Microsoft in exchange for $150 million. That kept the company out of bankruptcy court.

Then he trimmed the fat. After slashing 70 percent of the products from Apple's bloated product line, including laser printers, the Apple QuickTake digital camera, and the Newton PDA, he explained, "Focusing is about saying no."[33] Jobs saw that Apple was "executing wonderfully on many of the wrong things."[34] He added, "Deciding what not to do is as important as deciding what to do. It's true for companies, and it's true for products."[35] In turn, he drew four quadrants (Pro, Consumer, Desktop, and Laptop) and had Apple focus on just those four things. It was a total redirect from the vision at the time.

And Jobs's vision went beyond products. He also reimagined the team to ensure he could pursue the vision. He dumped the current board of directors and brought in a fresh team. "It's back to innovation," said Oracle CEO Larry Ellison, a member of the new board. "It's back to creativity. It's back to vision."[36]

That Zag was the first of many to come and launched the most innovative and profitable era in Apple's history. Propelled by the breakthrough technological release of the iPhone in 2007, Apple became the first American public company to be valued at more than $1 trillion.[37]

Amazon's Zag. As a Mature company, Amazon could stagnate by playing it safe, sticking to delivering a broad spectrum of merchandise via the web. But, instead of coasting into Legacy status, after twenty years they've retained their pioneering culture by Zagging and innovating like an aggressive Startup. From Alexa-enabled devices (controlling more than 4,000 smart home devices), Amazon Go retail stores (with no checkout required), and the advent of Prime Wardrobe (allowing customers to try before they buy), to creating a catalog of original programming on Prime Video, Amazon is ranked by customers number one in The American Customer Satisfaction Index year after year.[38]

Delighting customers through these constant innovations, coupled with their commitment to exceptionally seamless customer service, keeps Amazon striving for optimization efficiencies. "Even when they don't yet know it, customers want something better, and your desire to delight customers will drive you to invent on their behalf," as founder and CEO Jeff Bezos said. "No customer ever asked Amazon to create the Prime membership program, but it sure turns out they wanted it."[39]

Why does Amazon behave like a Startup rather than the Mature company that it is? In a letter to shareholders, Bezos explains why it's always "Day 1" at Amazon: "Day 2 is stasis. Followed by irrelevance. Followed by excruciating, painful decline. Followed by death. And *that* is why it is always Day 1. To be sure, this kind of decline would happen in extreme slow motion. An established company might harvest Day 2 for decades, but the final result would still come."[40] By constantly Zagging, Amazon stays young while it matures as a company.

The Legacy Zag

At the Legacy stage, your company has settled into its stride. Customers know, love, rely upon, and seek out your brand. The management team includes top talent in the field. The necessary systems and processes are in place to optimize operations. For publicly traded companies, stocks are paying consistent dividends. But, at risk is a loss of the original entrepreneurial spirit, which drove innovation and the taking of calculated risks.

A myopic view of the marketplace by leadership can cause blindness to emerging markets, customer trends, and breakthrough technological advances. Think Kodak. However, a decline can be avoided when a fresh vision is extended by leadership. Think Apple computers and the iPhone.

At the outset of this chapter we talked about how LEGO, as a Legacy company, Zagged back from the brink of bankruptcy into profitability under the leadership of CEO Jørgen Vig Knudstorp. In 2018, LEGO made the *Forbes* list of the Top 100 World's Most Valuable Brands,[41] which sure beats bankruptcy court, where they were headed before their Vision Zag. Here I want to look at another Legacy brand that made an effective Zag in the nick of time: Microsoft.

Microsoft's Zag. On April 4, 1975, Bill Gates and high school friend Paul Allen founded Microsoft. The right software and the right timing placed Microsoft at the epicenter of the PC revolution. When Gates stepped back from his lead role at Microsoft, he handed the "keys to the kingdom" to his successor, Steve Ballmer. Microsoft was a company that was at the top of its game—with nine out of ten PCs in the world running Windows.[42]

Over the next dozen or so years, what reporter Kurt Eichenwald called "Microsoft's lost decade,"[43] the company began its decline. Why? Largely, as Tom Warren says, because of Ballmer's "reliance on the Gates legacy and a lack of vision."[44] Just four years into Ballmer's tenure, Jim Allchin, a senior member of the leadership team, sent Ballmer and Gates this email: "I would buy a Mac today if I wasn't working at Microsoft. Apple did not lose their way."[45]

Under Ballmer, Microsoft lost its culture of innovation. According to David Seidman, a senior manager who worked under Ballmer, "Ballmer created a toxic culture, killed good products and shipped bad ones, and failed to anticipate industry trends. . . . Ballmer repeatedly killed products that went on to be huge businesses for other companies. Microsoft developed smartphones and tablets before Apple but didn't fund or outright killed multiple innovations."[46] We already mentioned Ballmer's lack of vision when it came to the iPhone. "There's no chance that the iPhone is going to get any significant market share," he said. "No chance."[47] Of course, the iPhone went on to produce more revenue than all of Microsoft's products combined.[48]

After Ballmer retired in 2014, Microsoft finally got its much-needed Vision Zag from new CEO Satya Nadella. Nadella was quick to identify the internal issues choking and holding back Microsoft's success. In his book, *Hit Refresh*, he reflects:

> The company was sick. Employees were tired. They were frustrated. They were fed up with losing and falling behind despite their grand plans and great ideas. They came to Microsoft with big dreams, but it felt like all they really did was deal with upper management, executing taxing processes, and bicker in meetings. . . . Like me, they'd come to Microsoft to change the world, but now were frustrated by our company's stalled growth. They were being wooed by competitors. Saddest of all, many felt the company was losing its soul.[49]

Nadella's fresh vision for the future was a departure from the status-quo behavior of his predecessor. Nadella Zagged from an era focusing on "devices and services" to that of a mobile and cloud connectivity future. Shortly after taking the helm as CEO, Nadella mapped out his vision in a memo to his colleagues, which included this perspective: "At our core, Microsoft is the productivity and platform company for the mobile-first and cloud-first world. We will reinvent productivity to empower every person and every organization on the planet to do more and achieve more."[50]

This Vision Zag breathed new life into the company, resulting in an increase in stock valuation from $36.35 when he took office, to tripling in value, trading above $113 per share at the end of 2018, just four years later.[51]

Let's not lose sight of the fact that when Nadella was handed the keys to the CEO suite, Microsoft was a Legacy company heading toward the land of Zombies. His Vision Zag both saved Microsoft and has charted a new course as a thriving organization. Moreover, because Microsoft was able to execute Nadella's new vision, on April 23, 2019, they became the third company in US history to reach a $1 trillion market valuation.[52]

The Zombie Zag

Simply put, Zombie companies are typically older companies vulnerable to defaulting on their debts. Many don't have enough profits to cover the interest payments on their loans. Even household brands who previously enjoyed Legacy status for decades are prime candidates for bankruptcy. According to a recent report, "The share of zombie companies in the US doubled between 2007 and 2015, rising to around 10% of all public companies."[53]

Just as Blockbuster failed to pivot quickly enough to ward off the threat of the Netflix model, Zombie companies failed to see the warning signs from disruptive innovators, which killed their viability. Their vision becomes that of preserving the status quo. And, while they are not legally dead, given their inability to attract new capital, they might as well be dead—unless market forces unexpectedly shift, or the company is resurrected by a Vision Zag.

United Record Pressing Company's Zag. For almost seven decades, the Nashville-based United Record vinyl pressing plant had been stamping out albums for artists like the Beatles and Bob Dylan. But in 1988, CD sales surpassed vinyl,[54] and vinyl records took a nosedive. By the mid-2000s, on the verge of becoming a Zombie, United responded by trimming their workforce and limited production to an anemic one shift. By all measures, they were mostly dead. That's when the unexpected happened.

The demand for vinyl shifted once again in 2008, this time by millennials and hipsters drawn to the album experience and the growing view of vinyl as a "collectible." New vinyl sales jumped 400 percent, from just under 4 million units in 2008 to 16 million units in 2017.[55] United staffed up from 40 to 150 employees and is running their pressing plant twenty-four hours a day, six days a week. Even so, "it is never enough to keep up with the demand."[56] In this case, the marketplace spoke so loudly, the company couldn't help but Zag in response.

Marvel's Zag. After several decades of saving the world with their superheroes, Marvel Entertainment Group couldn't save themselves from the clutches of defeat. In December 1996, they filed for bankruptcy protection after their stock value collapsed from $35.75 to $2.375 in just three years,[57] followed by a galactic battle between rich investors vying for control of Marvel's destiny. During these darkest of hours, Marvel auctioned the film rights to several of their top heroes, including Spider-Man, the X-Men, the Hulk, and the Fantastic Four.

After several years of legal wrangling, Marvel joined forces with ToyBiz, emerging from bankruptcy in June 1998 under a new name: Marvel Enterprises. Having sold the rights to their most popular superheroes, Marvel needed a new vision if they were to live to fight another day.

Their Vision Zag was comprised of three things. First, they decided to focus on movies rather than comic books—a radical change from their previous focus on pen and ink. Second, they leveraged several of their remaining crown jewels (such as Thor and Captain America) as collateral to secure a massive cash reserve of $525 million from Merrill Lynch.[58] This allowed them to bankroll their vision of ten movies over the next several years.

Third, given ToyBiz's expertise creating toys, Marvel Enterprises decided to make movies out of minor characters that few remembered, strategically picking superhero characters that would also make great toys. Which characters? Marvel wisely didn't leave the decision of selecting the action hero up to studio executives. Rather, they paid attention to the end-user—movie-going kids. More specifically, kids who'd likely purchase movie-themed merchandise to play with at home. "Marvel brought together groups of children, showed them pictures of its superheroes, and described their abilities and weapons," said author Ben Fritz, explaining how Marvel picked the winner. "Then they asked the kids which ones they would most like to play with as a toy. The overwhelming answer, to the surprise of many at Marvel, was Iron Man."[59]

Their Vision Zag of featuring lesser-known characters paid off. The first installment of *Iron Man* made $585.2 million worldwide, *Iron Man 2* made $623.9 million worldwide, while *Iron Man 3* grossed more than $1.2 billion at the box—bringing the three-movie franchise earnings to more than $2.4 billion, not including toys, soundtracks, and licensing.[60] No wonder Disney bought Marvel in 2009 for $4 billion.[61]

Marvel has since proved again and again their ability to take unknown superheroes from the pages of their threadbare comic books and turn them into box office and licensing gold. Take Black Panther, an overlooked character that had been created fifty years ago. When Panther pounced on the box office, global sales topped $1.3 billion, making it only the tenth movie to clear that benchmark.[62] Regarding their vision of creating movies conducive to mega-merchandise sales, Panther was estimated to "generate nearly $250 million in licensed merchandise sales in 2018."[63]

Today, Marvel's cinematic universe reigns supreme at the box office, with multiple billion-dollar franchises including Iron Man, the Avengers, Spider-Man, and X-Men.[64] And, as I write, Marvel's *Avengers: Endgame* had a record-breaking $1.2 billion worldwide ticket bonanza—in their first weekend of release.[65] All from a company that, to recall Miracle Max, was mostly dead.

The Dead Zag

Companies die. It happens every day. They run out of cash. They can't pay their employees, their suppliers, their creditors, and they fold. But even in this state, Zagging is possible, and many remarkable Lazarus companies have come back from the dead against all expectations. Here I'll tell just one story with two Dead Zags. Ninety million monthly users benefit from the first Zag,[66] and more than 10 million daily users[67] benefit from the second—including me and my company, and I bet many of you.

Stewart Butterfield is a fun-and-games kind of guy. That may stem from the fact he was raised by hippie parents. In 2002, he founded Ludicorp to build a computer role-playing game called Game Neverending. Ironically, it ended two years later. But the technology behind the game gave birth to Flickr, an online photo sharing and management app, which he sold to Yahoo on March 20, 2005, for a reported $35 million.[68] That's Zag number one.

Then in 2009, Butterfield launched a new tech venture, Tiny Speck, with offices in Canada and the US. Once again, he tried his hand at creating a multiplayer, browser-based game, Glitch. Four years and more than $10 million later, Glitch shut down because it couldn't generate a large enough audience.[69] But it wasn't entirely "Game Over" for Tiny Speck.

When Glitch flopped, the company disbanded except Butterfield and a few core members. They realized they might be able to pull one asset from the ashes, sort of like Butterfield had done before with Ludicorp's background technology when that company went belly-up. In this case, it was a communications platform the team had created to bridge the divide between their two offices. What if they could package that system for other companies with multiple offices and remote workers?[70] Ten million users and 85,000 companies call the answer to that question Slack, and they use the desktop and mobile apps every day.[71] Thanks to a Vision Zag, the side thing became the main thing.

Failure is normal. Success is what's rare. But one of the unfortunate reasons it's rare is because people give up when they hit a wall. The truth is that you might have a major idea right under your nose and not even know it. Sometimes our best assets can't be seen until failure removes the distractions. I love Slack for the ways that it improves the life of our team. But I also love it because it reminds us what it takes to win in business: a solution to a problem, simple and fun to use, that comes from a place of openness and optimism.

Butterfield Zagged not once, but twice—and ended up with Slack, a company valued at more than $1.12 billion

Sometimes our best assets can't be seen until failure removes the distractions.

within the first year and that hit $2 billion faster than any other Startup in history.[72] And here's the really cool part. Because Slack has been so financially successful, they, in turn, have made investments in more than forty other Startups.[73] The death of Tiny Speck produced Slack while giving life to dozens of Startups. That's the power of the Vision Zag.

ENVISION	**CHECK FOR CLARITY**	**CHECK FOR INSPIRATION**	**CHECK FOR PRACTICALITY**

SELL IT	**OVERCOME RESISTANCE**	**ZAG WHEN NECESSARY**

From everything we covered in Questions 3–9, a straightforward process emerges for taking a vision from inception to reality. Are you ready to make your vision come true?

The Permanent Zag

Zagging isn't a once-and-done thing that happens at a specific point in time. Nor is it a Hail Mary pass. Done right, the Vision Zag is an ongoing mindset. The vision-driven leader understands there's always a better future worth re-visioning. Every company encounters obstacles and opportunities to pivot, to zag, to adjust their vision. How and when is somewhat dependent upon where they fall on the Vision Arc. By keeping an eye on the horizon, leaders won't miss their moment in the sun—taking their companies to a future destination where they can really shine.

If you're still tempted to question whether it's too late for your company to rebound or to forge a new course, look no further than Amazon, Apple, Microsoft, and Marvel for inspiration. In all four cases, we see the transformative power of a vibrant, compelling vision at work, enabling them to change the trajectory of their businesses for the better. They also know that their vision must always be renewed if they are to thrive and grow. And that's why your company needs a vision-driven leader. So the only question at this point is, Are you ready?

Are You Ready?

Preparing for the Journey Ahead

Some men see things as they are and say, "Why?" I
dream of things that never were, and say, "Why not?"

GEORGE BERNARD SHAW[1]

For several years now, economists and other observers have noted America's lack of economic energy, especially as revealed in the declining number of new startups. Entrepreneurialism is down. Innovation increasingly happens within existing firms. And there's less economic churn, which means overall slower growth. Some representative headlines include these:

- "The Mysterious Death of Entrepreneurship in America"
- "Behind the Productivity Plunge: Fewer Startups"

- "Start-Ups Aren't Cool Anymore"
- "American Entrepreneurship Is Actually Vanishing"
- "America's Startup Scene Is Looking Anemic"
- "The US Startup Is Disappearing"
- "Dynamism in Retreat"[2]

Theories and explanations abound. Some say the cause is increased regulation. Others point to lower personal savings with which to start new companies. Like any complex situation, there are probably many contributing factors, but any accounting would be incomplete if it didn't factor in a lack of vision.

Tellingly, when *Inc.* magazine asked its readers which of several different factors prevented would-be entrepreneurs from launching, the two answers most selected were not competitive barriers, lack of skills, the high rate of business failure, or taxes and regulations. Rather, they were "I don't have an idea" (40 percent of respondents) and "I don't think I could raise enough money" (48 percent of respondents).[3] Those are vision problems. Either would-be entrepreneurs have no vision, or it's not compelling enough to sell investors.

You have to take the next step. The world needs your vision.

My hope is that this book can help you, as a vision-driven leader, change the statistics. Are you ready? It's the final question of the book and in some ways the most important.

In part 1, I showed you the vital importance of vision for leaders who want to build thriving, successful businesses. In part 2, I showed you how to create a compelling Vision Script for your organization and enroll your team. In part 3, I've shown you how to overcome obstacles and pivot at whatever stage you currently find yourself. But you have to take the next step. The world needs your vision.

Missed Opportunities

In 1876, William Orten, the president of Western Union, was contacted by Alexander Graham Bell with an offer to purchase Bell's patent of the telephone for $100,000, roughly $2 million today. Western Union commanded 90 percent of the telegraph business, which in its day was a considerable step up from homing pigeons and the Pony Express. But the telephone represented a whole new breakthrough.

Orten—like Kodak and the digital camera or all the investors who passed on the idea that became Zappos—didn't see it. Dismissing Bell's invention, Orten wrote him a letter, saying, "While it is a very interesting novelty, we have come to the conclusion that it has no commercial possibilities. . . . What use could this company make of an electrical toy?"[4] About thirty years after Orten's rejection of Bell's invention, Western Union was taken over by a company with bigger vision, the American Telephone & Telegraph Company, which most of us know as AT&T. Ouch. Those opportunities don't come back, do they?

When fresh, even crazy visions for companies like Airbnb, Uber, eBay, DoorDash, Dollar Shave Club, and Amazon came along, plenty of people saw them as far-fetched and absurd. Before Amazon became the behemoth that it is today, it was viewed by Wall Street analysts with "extreme skepticism."[5] One journalist said Amazon "will never be the high-growth, wildly profitable, super-efficient company of Internet lore. The only place that company lives is in the history books, and in the powerful imagination of Jeff Bezos."[6] Who's laughing now?

The Road to Oblivion

During my lifetime I've watched Legacy companies with commanding global footprints, who employed tens of thousands of workers and who possessed stellar brand recognition, drift into oblivion or, almost as bad, irrelevance.

Consider Kodak, Blockbuster, Nokia, Borders Books and Music, Radio Shack, Circuit City, Toys"Я"Us, Atari, Eastern Airlines, Tower Records, Woolworth's, Swissair, the Sharper Image, Sunbeam Products, Pan Am, Lionel Corporation, Atkins, J. C. Penney, Commodore Computers, Bethlehem Steel, Motorola, Kmart, and Sears—to name just a few. What happened? Why did these major brands slumber, slump, and slide into crisis, or worse?

Any number of factors played a part, including massive economic and technological shifts. But another answer underlies them all: at key moments in their organization's life, they lacked vision. For a host of reasons, they failed to assess their present reality and then look beyond to anticipate where they *could* and *should* be. Or, if they took that step, they failed to execute on their vision.

As Arthur C. Clarke wrote, "With monotonous regularity, apparently competent men have laid down the law about what is technically possible or impossible—and have been proved wrong, sometimes while the ink was scarcely dry from their pens." Why? He said it all comes down to "failures of imagination" and "failures of nerve."[7]

Don't forget restaurateur Danny Meyer's questions from earlier: "How can we become the company that would put us out of business?" and "What might this predator look like and why would it have an advantage over us?" Someone is asking that about your business right now. You need to answer before they do.

Your Move

Answering the final question—Are you ready?—involves asking several others, starting with, What kind of leader are you? Are you allergic to taking risks? Are you happy with the status quo? Do you tend to follow an existing map rather than charting new territory? Are you focused on the bottom line rather than the horizon? Is this because you haven't (until now) seen the value of doing "the vision thing"?

If so, you have a lot in common with a manager like President George H. W. Bush. Don't fret. There's still time to become a vision-driven leader by applying the Vision Scripting method we've discussed. That's a decision only you can make.

On the other hand, Are you restless with doing the same thing year after year? Are you concerned about missing future opportunities? Are you comfortable defining and setting a direction? Do you tend to keep an eye on the horizon rather than on the moment? Great. It's time to feed your inner JFK. The tools in this book will help you identify and execute your moon shot.

Every Vision Script is unique, but I've learned that every new initiative presents a predictable set of challenges. I don't care if you are launching a business, leading a division within an organization, or taking a promotion as the CEO of a company, you have to take five steps to succeed in developing and delivering a Vision Script that will define your future.

*1. **Schedule it.*** Many people skip this step. Don't. There is something that happens when you set aside the necessary time. It's a way of focusing your intention and clarifying what you want to accomplish. Block the time on your calendar and start pulling together whatever you need to help you answer Question 3: What Do You Want? Launching a new vision is tough, and you probably have more on your plate than you can say grace over. How in the world could you make time for one more thing? It's better to ask, How could you not? The Vision Scripter at VisionDrivenLeader.com will help you make the most efficient use of this time.

*2. **Get the necessary input.*** One thing I learned from my dad is that it's possible to do almost anything if you are willing to surround yourself with good counsel. While creating a compelling Vision Script is your responsibility as the leader, inviting several members of your leadership team to embark on that journey with you—or at least be available to give you early feedback—makes the task less daunting.

*3. **Trust the process.*** This is huge. Usually, when I take on something really big, I have only a foggy idea of how to get from point A to point B. I have enough light to take the next step, and that is usually enough. When I take that step, the next thing I need either shows up on its own or I become aware of how to get it. But that wouldn't have occurred if I didn't trust it would and gotten under way.

Remember, you're going off the map into new and unfamiliar territory. You won't have all of the answers pinned down at first. Vision Scripting is a discovery process. Work through your answers to the questions posed in part 2:

- What Do You Want?
- Is It Clear?
- Does It Inspire?
- Is It Practical?
- Can You Sell It?

As you do, your vision will take shape.

4. Tweak as you go. Your Vision Script is not a once-and-done thing. As I said earlier, you're not Moses coming down the mountain with stone tablets that can't be changed. It's your vision. You have the freedom and flexibility to rethink, revise, and recast based on any number of factors, including input from your team.

There are no vision police waiting to write you a ticket for failure to nail it on the first pass. And you'll never get to the second or third draft if you don't write the first one. Knowing that you can tweak along the way takes the pressure off of trying to be perfect with your initial version.

5. Go ahead and launch. At some point, you have to sell the vision and then begin executing. As I coach leaders, I often encounter a reluctance to finalize the plan and put it to work. They keep fiddling with it, hoping to get it perfect. Resist the temptation. "A good plan violently executed now is better than a perfect plan executed next week," as General George Patton once said.[8] Perfection is just another way of saying procrastination. And you don't have time for that. Your team is waiting to see what you see.

Perfection is just another way of saying procrastination. And you don't have time for that. Your team is waiting to see what you **see.**

The Vision-Driven Future

As we've seen in story after story, vision-driven leaders breathe life into dead or dying companies (think Marvel). They innovate new cutting-edge products (think Apple). They create businesses that never existed before (think Airbnb). And they give their employees the direction and focus necessary to infuse their culture with fresh energy and purpose (think Microsoft).

In my own life as an entrepreneur and executive, I've seen vision as the essential ingredient in my leadership: once when I was missing it and lost my business; and many times since when vision propelled me forward to achieve more than I knew I was capable of.

So, back to our question: Are you ready? Wouldn't it be exciting to take your people in the bold new direction you want them to go? Wouldn't you love to see your team energized by what the future holds for you and your organization? You can. It's your turn to lead and win with vision. Waiting feels safe, but waiting kills vision. Where will you take your team next?

Jumpstart Your Vision Script

The Vision Scripter is a simple, interactive system that makes crafting your Vision Script fast and easy.
Try it free at VisionDrivenLeader.com

Notes

Question 1 Are You a Leader or a Manager?

1. John F. Kennedy, remarks in the Assembly Hall at the Paulskirche in Frankfurt, June 25, 1963, https://www.jfklibrary.org/asset-viewer /archives/JFKWHA/1963/JFKWHA-199/JFKWHA-199.

2. Craig Allen, *Eisenhower and the Mass Media* (Chapel Hill: University of North Carolina Press, 1993), 163.

3. John F. Kennedy, "Special Message to the Congress on Urgent National Needs," delivered before the joint session of Congress, May 25, 1961, https://www.jfklibrary.org/asset-viewer/archives/JFKPOF/034 /JFKPOF-034-030.

4. Yanek Mieczkowski, *Eisenhower's Sputnik Moment* (Ithaca: Cornell University Press, 2013), 268.

5. J. D. Hunley, ed., *The Birth of NASA* (Washington, DC: NASA History Office, 1993), xxvi.

6. Roger D. Launius, "Public Opinion Polls and Perceptions of US Human Spaceflight," *Science Direct*, PDF accessed June 11, 2019, https:// www.sciencedirect.com/science/article/abs/pii/S0265964603000390.

7. Kennedy, "Special Message to the Congress on Urgent National Needs."

8. Robert Ajemian, "Where Is the Real George Bush?," *Time*, January 26, 1987, http://content.time.com/time/magazine/article/0,9171,963 342,00.html.

9. Margaret Garrard Warner, "Bush Battles the 'Wimp Factor,'" *Newsweek*, October 19, 1987, https://www.newsweek.com/bush-battles-wimp -factor-207008.

10. Stephen Knott, "George H. W. Bush: Campaigns and Elections," MillerCenter.org, retrieved February 18, 2019, https://millercenter.org/president/bush/campaigns-and-elections.

11. Seth Godin, *Tribes* (New York: Penguin Group, 2008), 137.

12. Noel Tichy and Ram Charan, "Speed, Simplicity, Self-Confidence: An Interview with Jack Welch," *Harvard Business Review*, September–October 1989, https://hbr.org/1989/09/speed-simplicity-self-confidence-an-interview-with-jack-welch.

13. Warren Bennis, *On Becoming a Leader* (Philadelphia: Basic Books, 2009), 42.

14. Bill Jerome and Curtis Powell, *The Disposable Visionary* (Santa Barbara: Praeger, 2016), xv.

15. Sheryl Sandberg, "The Scaling of Vision," Stanford Technology Ventures Program, April 22, 2009, https://ecorner.stanford.edu/video/the-scaling-of-vision.

16. You might, for instance, have contracts or investment requirements that make a longer time frame necessary. Similarly, the complexity or scope of your business might require more long-range visioneering.

17. Jeffrey A. Kottler, *What You Don't Know About Leadership but Probably Should* (New York: Oxford University Press, 2018), 11.

18. Bonnie Hagemann, Simon Vetter, and John Maketa, *Leading with Vision* (Boston: Nicholas Brealey, 2017), xiv.

19. Heriminia Ibarra, *Act Like a Leader, Think Like a Leader* (Boston: Harvard Business Review Press, 2015), 43. Curiously, Ibarra adds that "women are more likely than men to rate a shortfall on this dimension" (195). If that's true, it strikes me as a powerful opportunity and source of competitive advantage for women leaders who excel at vision, or desire to do so. See Herminia Ibarra and Otilia Obodaru, "Women and the Vision Thing," *Harvard Business Review*, January 2009, https://hbr.org/2009/01/women-and-the-vision-thing.

20. Suzanna Bates, *All the Leader You Can Be* (New York: McGraw-Hill, 2016), 45.

Question 2 What Difference Does Vision Make?

1. Yogi Berra, *The Yogi Book* (New York: Workman, 2010), 132.

2. "George Eastman," Kodak.com, https://www.kodak.com/US/en/corp/aboutus/heritage/georgeeastman/default.htm.

3. Claudia H. Deutsch, "At Kodak, Some Old Things Are New Again," *New York Times*, May 2, 2008, https://www.nytimes.com/2008/05/02/technology/02kodak.html.

4. Mary Elaine Ramos, "Kodak: The Biggest Corporate Casualty in the Digital Age?," *International Business Times*, January 25, 2012, https://www.ibtimes.com.au/kodak-biggest-corporate-casualty-digital-age-1292792.

5. Robert Strohmeyer, "The 7 Worst Tech Predictions of All Time," *PCWorld*, December 31, 2008, https://www.pcworld.com/article/155984 /worst_tech_predictions.html.

6. David Sheff, "The Playboy Interview: Steve Jobs," *Playboy*, February 1985, http://reprints.longform.org/playboy-interview-steve-jobs.

7. Brent Schlender and Rick Tetzeli, *Becoming Steve Jobs* (New York: Crown, 2015), 408.

8. Sheff, "The Playboy Interview: Steve Jobs."

9. Schlender and Tetzeli, *Becoming Steve Jobs*, 58.

10. Caroline Cakebread, "People Will Take 1.2 Trillion Digital Photos This Year—Thanks to Smartphones," *Business Insider*, August 31, 2017, https://www.businessinsider.com.au/12-trillion-photos-to-be-taken-in -2017-thanks-to-smartphones-chart-2017-8.

11. Hunter Schwarz, "How Many Photos Have Been Taken Ever?," *BuzzFeed*, September 24, 2012, https://www.buzzfeed.com/hunterschwarz /how-many-photos-have-been-taken-ever-6zgv.

12. See this article at Quote Investigator: https://quoteinvestigator .com/2012/09/27/invent-the-future.

13. Linda Musthaler, "30 Years Later, Compaq Leaves a Legacy That Benefits You," *NetworkWorld*, November 9, 2012, https://www.network world.com/article/2161331/30-years-later-compaq-leaves-a-legacy-that -benefits-you.html.

14. Musthaler, "30 Years Later, Compaq Leaves a Legacy That Bene-fits You."

15. Saul Hansell, "Compaq to Buy Digital Equipment for $9.6 Billion," *New York Times*, January 27, 1998, http://movies2.nytimes.com/library /cyber/week/012798digital-side.html.

16. Musthaler, "30 Years Later, Compaq Leaves a Legacy That Bene-fits You."

17. Hansell, "Compaq to Buy Digital Equipment for $9.6 Billion."

18. Dave Farquhar, "Why Did Compaq Fail?," *Silicon Underground*, March 15, 2018, https://dfarq.homeip.net/why-did-compaq-fail.

19. Scott Pendleton, "Compaq's Ride from Casualty to Conqueror of the PC Market," *Christian Science Monitor*, February 14, 1995, https:// www.csmonitor.com/1995/0214/14081.html.

20. Farquhar, "Why Did Compaq Fail?"

21. Mikey Campbell, "Jawbone Reportedly Shuttering Business Amidst Financial Turmoil, New Health Startup to Rise from Ashes," AppleInsider.com, July 6, 2017, https://appleinsider.com/articles/17/07 /06/jawbone-reportedly-shuttering-business-amidst-financial-turmoil -new-health-startup-to-rise-from-ashes.

22. Reuters, "Jawbone's Demise a Case of 'Death by Overfunding' in Sil-icon Valley," CNBC.com, July 10, 2017, https://www.reuters.com/article

/us-jawbone-failure/jawbones-demise-a-case-of-death-by-overfunding-in-silicon-valley-idUSKBN19V0BS.

23. "Fitness Wearables Maker Jawbone Goes into Liquidation," News.com.au, July 11, 2017, https://www.news.com.au/finance/business/technology/fitness-wearables-maker-jawbone-goes-into-liquidation/news-story/737dc3e64dd0907c021c0a40f841f652.

24. Carmine Gallo, "Steve Jobs: Get Rid of the Crappy Stuff," *Forbes*, May 16, 2011, https://www.forbes.com/sites/carminegallo/2011/05/16/steve-jobs-get-rid-of-the-crappy-stuff/#68a927f57145.

25. Gallo, "Steve Jobs: Get Rid of the Crappy Stuff."

26. Gallo, "Steve Jobs: Get Rid of the Crappy Stuff."

27. Oliver Kmia, "Why Kodak Died and Fujifilm Thrived," Petapixel.com, October 19, 2018, https://petapixel.com/2018/10/19/why-kodak-died-and-fujifilm-thrived-a-tale-of-two-film-companies/.

28. Kmia, "Why Kodak Died and Fujifilm Thrived."

29. James M. Kouzes and Barry Posner, "To Lead, Create a Shared Vision," *Harvard Business Review*, January 2009, https://hbr.org/2009/01/to-lead-create-a-shared-vision.

30. Ibarra, *Act Like a Leader*, 43–44.

31. Heike Bruch and Sumantra Ghoshal, "Beware the Busy Manager," *Harvard Business Review*, February 2002, https://hbr.org/2002/02/beware-the-busy-manager.

32. Carmine Gallo, "18,000 Pages of NASA Archives Uncover JFK's Speech Strategy That Inspired the Moon Landing," *Forbes*, October 11, 2018, https://www.forbes.com/sites/carminegallo/2018/10/11/18000-pages-of-nasa-archives-uncovers-jfks-speech-strategy-that-inspired-the-moon-landing.

33. Jon Reynolds and Ben Medlock, "SwiftKey Is Joining Microsoft," *SwiftKey Blog*, February 3, 2016, https://blog.swiftkey.com/microsoft-acquires-swiftkey.

34. Harry Shum, "Microsoft Acquires SwiftKey in Support of Re-inventing Productivity Ambition," *Official Microsoft Blog*, February 3, 2016, https://blogs.microsoft.com/blog/2016/02/03/microsoft-acquires-swiftkey-in-support-of-re-inventing-productivity-ambition.

35. Ingrid Lunden and Mike Butcher, "Microsoft Confirms SwiftKey Acquisition (for $250M in Cash)," TechCrunch.com, February 3, 2016, https://techcrunch.com/2016/02/03/microsoft-confirms-swiftkey-acquisition-for-250m-in-cash.

36. Aamna Mohdin, "SwiftKey's Co-founder Sold His Shares for a Bicycle—and Missed Out on a Share of $250 Million," Quartz.com, February 4, 2016, https://qz.com/610144/swiftkeys-co-founder-sold-his-shares-for-a-bicycle-and-missed-out-on-a-share-of-250-million.

37. "Henry Ford Changes the World, 1908," EyeWitness to History, www.eyewitnesstohistory.com/ford.htm.

38. Henry Ford, *My Life and Work* (New York: Doubleday, 1923), 73.

Question 3 What Do You Want?

1. Alan Jackson and David Byers, "Bob Dylan Says Barack Obama Is 'Changin' America," *London Times*, June 5, 2008.

2. Karl Taro Greenfeld, "Blind to Failure," *Time*, June 18, 2001, http://content.time.com/time/world/article/0,8599,2047596,00.html.

3. Michael D'Estries, "A Warming Mount Everest Is Giving Up Its Dead," MNN.com, March 28, 2019, https://www.mnn.com/earth-matters/climate-weather/blogs/warming-mount-everest-giving-its-dead.

4. Christine Wang, "Erik Weihenmayer: The Only Way to Climb Everest Is to Go Do It," CNBC.com, April 4, 2016, https://www.cnbc.com/2016/04/04/erik-weihenmayer-the-only-way-to-climb-everest-is-to-go-do-it.html.

5. Greenfeld, "Blind to Failure."

6. Peter Economy, "5 Essential Questions for Entrepreneurs," *Inc.*, September 5, 2013, https://www.inc.com/peter-economy/5-essential-questions-entrepreneurs.html.

7. Cited in Steven Johnson, *Farsighted* (New York: Riverhead, 2018), 81.

8. Jenny Blake, *Pivot* (New York: Portfolio, 2016), 55.

9. Newsweek Special Edition, "Michael Jordan Didn't Make Varsity—At First," *Newsweek*, October 17, 2015, https://www.newsweek.com/missing-cut-382954.

10. Newsweek Special Edition, "Michael Jordan Didn't Make Varsity."

11. Roger Connors and Tom Smith, *The Wisdom of Oz* (New York: Penguin, 2014), 115.

12. Rachel Gillett, "How Walt Disney, Oprah Winfrey, and 19 Other Successful People Rebounded After Getting Fired," *Inc.*, October 7, 2015, https://www.inc.com/business-insider/21-successful-people-who-rebounded-after-getting-fired.html.

13. "Celebs Who Went from Failures to Success Stories," CBSNews.com, https://www.cbsnews.com/pictures/celebs-who-went-from-failures-to-success-stories.

14. Burt Nanus, *Visionary Leadership* (San Francisco: Jossey-Bass, 1992), 31.

15. Warren Berger, *The Book of Beautiful Questions* (New York: Bloomsbury, 2018), 173.

16. Berger, *Book of Beautiful Questions*, 173–75.

17. Zach St. George, "Curiosity Depends on What You Already Know," *Nautilus*, February 25, 2016, http://nautil.us/issue/33/attraction/curiosity-depends-on-what-you-already-know.

18. See David C. Robertson, *Brick by Brick* (New York: Crown Business, 2013), 145–50.

19. Herminia Ibarra makes the same point in *Act Like a Leader*, 42.

Question 4 Is It Clear?

1. Beau Lotto, *Deviate* (London: Weidenfeld & Nicolson, 2017), 296.

2. Heiki Bruch and Bernd Vogel, *Fully Charged* (Boston: Harvard Business Review Press, 2011), 88.

3. Hagemann et al., *Leading with Vision*, 55–56.

4. The concrete/abstract distinction is a fairly common way to speak about language. The implicit/explicit distinction is adapted from Michael Polanyi's tacit/explicit distinction. See, e.g., Polanyi's *Personal Knowledge* (Chicago: University of Chicago Press, 1962) and *The Tacit Dimension* (Chicago: University of Chicago Press, 1966).

5. Blake, *Pivot*, 60. Blake is describing personal career visions, but I find her insight applicable to larger organizational visions as well.

6. Karen Martin, *Clarity First* (New York: McGraw-Hill, 2018), 18–26.

7. Proverbs 15:22.

8. Blake, *Pivot*, 56.

9. Martin, *Clarity First*, 30.

Question 5 Does It Inspire?

1. Richard Sheridan, *Chief Joy Officer* (New York: Portfolio, 2018), 87.

2. Basharat Peer, "The Girl Who Wanted to Go to School," *New Yorker*, October 10, 2012, https://www.newyorker.com/news/news-desk/the-girl-who-wanted-to-go-to-school.

3. Peer, "The Girl Who Wanted to Go to School."

4. Kate Douglas and Anna Poletti, *Life Narratives and Youth Culture* (London: Palgrave Macmillan, 2016), 207.

5. Owais Tohid, "My Conversations with Malala Yousafzai, the Girl Who Stood Up to the Taliban," *Christian Science Monitor*, October 11, 2012, https://www.csmonitor.com/World/Global-News/2012/1011/My-conversations-with-Malala-Yousafzai-the-girl-who-stood-up-to-the-Taliban.

6. Malala Yousafzai, "Malala's Story," Malala Fund, https://www.malala.org/malalas-story.

7. "Angelina Jolie Donates $200,000 to Malala Fund," *HuffPost*, April 5, 2013, https://www.huffpost.com/entry/angelina-jolie-malala-charity_n_3019303. "How We Work Grant: The Malala Fund," Bill & Melinda Gates Foundation, https://www.gatesfoundation.org/How-We-Work/Quick-Links/Grants-Database/Grants/2016/12/OPP1166109. Katie Reilly, "Apple Is Partnering with Malala's Non-Profit to Educate

More Than 100,000 Girls," *Time*, January 22, 2018, https://time.com
/5112439/apple-malala-fund.

8. Linda Poon, "Now This Is an Example of Truly Educational Radio,"
NPR.org, February 18, 2015, https://www.npr.org/sections/goatsandsoda
/2015/02/18/387027766/now-this-is-an-example-of-truly-educational
-radio.

9. Mary Bellis, "Hailing: History of the Taxi," ThoughtCo.com,
February 24, 2019, https://www.thoughtco.com/hailing-history-of-the
-taxi-1992541.

10. Schaller Consulting, "The New York City Taxicab Fact Book,"
http://schallerconsult.com/taxi.

11. Dan Blystone, "The Story of Uber," Investopedia.com, March 31,
2019, https://www.investopedia.com/articles/personal-finance/111015
/story-uber.asp.

12. Hamish McRae, "Facebook, Airbnb, Uber, and the Unstoppable
Rise of the Content Non-Generators," *Independent*, May 5, 2015, https://
www.independent.co.uk/news/business/comment/hamish-mcrae/face
book-airbnb-uber-and-the-unstoppable-rise-of-the-content-non-genera
tors-10227207.html.

13. Duncan J. Watts, *Everything Is Obvious* (New York: Crown, 2011).

14. "Monthly Number of Uber's Active Users Worldwide from 2016
to 2018 (in Millions)," Statista.com, retrieved April 1, 2019, https://www
.statista.com/statistics/833743/us-users-ride-sharing-services.

15. Kathryn Gessner, "Uber vs. Lyft: Who's Tops in the Battle of U.S.
Rideshare Companies," Second Measure, July 19, 2019, https://second
measure.com/datapoints/rideshare-industry-overview. See also Greg
Bensinger and Chester Dawdon, "Toyota Investing $500 Million in Uber
in Driverless-Car Pact," *Wall Street Journal*, August 27, 2018, https://www
.wsj.com/articles/toyota-investing-500-million-in-uber-in-driverless-car
-pact-1535393774.

16. Press Release, "Apple Reinvents the Phone with iPhone," Apple.com,
January 9, 2007, https://www.apple.com/newsroom/2007/01/09Apple
-Reinvents-the-Phone-with-iPhone/.

17. Press Release, "Apple Reinvents the Phone with iPhone."

18. Stephanie Buck, "11 Hilarious Naysayers Who Criticized the First
iPhone 10 Years Ago," Timeline.com, January 6, 2017, https://timeline
.com/iphone-skeptics-611ea9de5d07.

19. PC World Editors, "The iPhone: Lots to Love, but Flaws Too," *PC
World*, June 30, 2007, https://www.pcworld.com/article/133639/article
.html.

20. Connie Guglielmo, "10 Years Ago Today: Remembering Steve Jobs
Make iPhone History," CNET.com, January 9, 2017, https://www.cnet

.com/news/iphone-at-10-apple-steve-jobs-make-iphone-history-remem bering/.

21. Seth Porges, "The Futurist: We Predict the iPhone Will Bomb," Techcrunch.com, July 6, 2007, https://techcrunch.com/2007/06/07/the -futurist-we-predict-the-iphone-will-bomb.

22. Press Release, "Apple Celebrates One Billion iPhones," Apple.com, July 27, 2016, https://www.apple.com/newsroom/2016/07/apple-celebrates -one-billion-iphones.

23. "Nobody loved it . . ." is a line I've heard attributed to gospel music impresario Bill Gaither.

24. David Sax, *The Revenge of Analog* (New York: Public Affairs, 2016).

25. See Nassim Nicholas Taleb's discussion in *Fooled by Randomness*, 2nd ed. (New York: Random House, 2005).

26. Aly Juma, "5 Lessons from the Wright Brothers and the Power of Purpose," *Art Plus Marketing*, November 7, 2017, https://artplusmarket ing.com/5-lessons-from-the-wright-brothers-and-the-power-of-purpose -a9f49af89330.

27. See, for instance, chap. 2 of Israel M. Kirzner's *Competition and Entrepreneurship* (Chicago: University of Chicago Press, 1978).

28. Sheridan, *Chief Joy Officer*, 89.

Question 6 Is It Practical?

1. "Evelyn Berezin: 2015 Fellow," Computer History Museum, https:// www.computerhistory.org/fellowawards/hall/evelyn-berezin. Emphasis added.

2. Matthew G. Kirschenbaum, *Track Changes* (Cambridge: Belknap, 2016), 149–55. See also Robert D. McFadden, "Evelyn Berezin, 93, Dies; Built the First True Word Processor," *New York Times*, December 10, 2018, https://www.nytimes.com/2018/12/10/obituaries/evelyn-berezin -dead.html; and Jack Schofield, "Evelyn Berezin obituary," *Guardian*, December 19, 2018, https://www.theguardian.com/technology/2018/dec /19/evelyn-berezin-obituary.

3. Gwyn Headley, "Why Is This Woman Not Famous?," *From Harlech & London*, December 20, 2010, http://fotolibrarian.fotolibra.com/?p=466.

4. From a July 17, 2013, comment Berezin left on Headley's post.

5. Michael Schrage, "R&D Won't Succeed If It Ignores the CEO's Vision," *Harvard Business Review*, April 13, 2015, https://hbr.org/2015 /04/rt-succeed-if-it-ignores-the-ceos-vision.

6. Tommy Caldwell, *The Push* (New York: Viking, 2017), 179.

7. Caldwell, *The Push*, 194.

8. Heike Bruch and Sumantra Ghoshal, "Beware the Busy Manager," *Harvard Business Review*, February 2002, 63.

9. Brent D. Peterson and Gaylan W. Nielson, *Fake Work* (New York: Simon Spotlight, 2009).

10. Meng Zhu, "Why We Procrastinate When We Have Long Deadlines," *Harvard Business Review*, September 4, 2018, https://hbr.org/2018/08/why-we-procrastinate-when-we-have-long-deadlines.

11. In *Free to Focus*, I show you how to protect this time using my Ideal Week planning tool.

12. Caldwell, *The Push*, 316.

13. Jennifer Riel and Roger L. Martin, *Creating Great Choices* (Boston: Harvard Business School Press, 2017), 5.

14. Riel and Martin, *Creating Great Choices*, 5–8.

15. Jennifer Luna, "Jane Chen: Be Courageous Because You Will Fail," Insights by Stanford Business, July 31, 2017, https://www.gsb.stanford.edu/insights/jane-chen-be-courageous-because-you-will-fail. See also Karen Weise, "Jane Chen: A Simple, Effective Way to Reduce Infant Mortality," *Bloomberg Business Week*, April 11, 2016, https://www.bloomberg.com/features/2016-design/a/jane-chen.

16. Helmuth von Moltke, *Moltke on the Art of War*, ed. Daniel J. Hughes (New York: Presidio, 1993), 92.

17. Megan Hyatt Miller, "How to Nail Your Goals with This Simple Secret," MichaelHyatt.com, May 27, 2016, https://michaelhyatt.com/nail-your-goals.

18. Caldwell, *The Push*, 233.

19. Laurie Beth Jones, *The Path* (New York: Hyperion, 1996), 86.

20. Andre Lavoie, "How to Engage Employees through Your Company Vision Statement," *Entrepreneur*, March 21, 2017, https://www.entrepreneur.com/article/290803.

21. Bill Murphy Jr., "Working with Millennials? Gallup Says Everything You Think You Know Is Wrong," *Inc.*, May 12, 2016, https://www.inc.com/bill-murphy-jr/working-with-millennials-gallup-says-everything-you-think-you-know-is-wrong.html.

22. Richard Fry, "Millennials Are the Largest Generation in the U.S. Labor Force," *Pew Research Center*, April 11, 2018, https://www.pewresearch.org/fact-tank/2018/04/11/millennials-largest-generation-us-labor-force.

23. "How Millennials Want to Work and Live," Everwise.com, February 8, 2017, https://www.geteverwise.com/company-culture/how-millennials-want-to-work-and-live.

24. Cited in Scott E. Page, *The Diversity Bonus* (Princeton: Princeton University Press, 2017), 52.

25. Andre Lavoie, "How to Establish a Vision Statement Employees Will Get Behind," *Entrepreneur*, April 21, 2015, https://www.entrepreneur.com/article/245249.

Question 7 Can You Sell It?

1. Guy Kawasaki, *Selling the Dream* (New York: HarperCollins, 1991), 4.

2. Thomas Sowell, "The End of Montgomery Ward," *Controversial Essays* (Stanford: Hoover Institution Press, 2002), 36–38.

3. Gary Hoover, "General Robert Wood: The Forgotten Man Who Changed Sears and the World," Archbridge Institute, August 22, 2018, https://www.archbridgeinstitute.org/general-robert-wood/.

4. Andy Stanley, *Visioneering*, rev. ed. (New York: Multnomah, 2016), 125.

5. Dan Ciampa, "What CEOs Get Wrong about Vision and How to Get It Right," *MIT Sloan Management Review*, Fall 2017, https://sloan review.mit.edu/article/what-ceos-get-wrong-about-vision-and-how-to -get-it-right/.

6. Lotto, *Deviate*, 296.

7. James 1:19 NIV.

8. https://twitter.com/andystanley/status/103841035108630528.

9. Lou Solomon, "The Top Complaints from Employees about Their Leaders," *Harvard Business Review*, June 24, 2015, https://hbr.org/2015 /06/the-top-complaints-from-employees-about-their-leaders.

Question 8 How Should You Face Resistance?

1. Steven Church, "Mike Tyson's Ear Fixation, and Mine," *Salon*, July 6, 2013, https://www.salon.com/2013/07/05/mike_tysons_ear_fix ation_and_mine.

2. Mike Wall, "FAQ: Alan Shepard's Historic Flight as First American in Space," Space.com, May 4, 2011, https://www.space.com/11562-nasa -american-spaceflight-alan-shepard-spaceflight-faq.html.

3. Nick Heath, "NASA's Unsung Heroes," *TechRepublic*, July 20, 2018, https://www.techrepublic.com/article/nasas-unsung-heroes-the -apollo-coders-who-put-men-on-the-moon.

4. Heath, "NASA's Unsung Heroes."

5. John F. Kennedy, address at Rice University on the Nation's Space Effort, September 12, 1962, https://www.jfklibrary.org/learn/about-jfk /historic-speeches/address-at-rice-university-on-the-nations-space-effort.

6. Sheridan, *Chief Joy Officer*, 89.

7. Bob Allen, "NASA Langley Research Center's Contributions to the Apollo Program," NASA.gov, April 22, 2008, https://www.nasa.gov /centers/langley/news/factsheets/Apollo.html.

8. Kirschenbaum, *Track Changes*, 150.

9. Leander Kahney, *Tim Cook* (New York: Portfolio, 2019), 102–6.

10. Ron Adner, "How the Kindle Stomped Sony, or, Why Good Solutions Beat Great Products," *Fast Company*, February 29, 2012, https://

www.fastcompany.com/1669160/how-the-kindle-stomped-Sony-or-why
-good-solutions-beat-great-products.

11. "The Etiology of Puerperal Fever," *JAMA*, April 15, 1933, https://
jamanetwork.com/journals/jama/article-abstract/242574.

12. Irvine Loudon, *The Tragedy of Childbed Fever* (Oxford: Oxford
University Press, 2000), 6.

13. Howard Markel, "In 1850, Ignaz Semmelweis Saved Lives with Three
Words: Wash Your Hands," *PBS*, May 15, 2015, https://www.pbs.org/news
hour/health/ignaz-semmelweis-doctor-prescribed-hand-washing. See also
Ignaz Semmelweis and K. Codell Carter, *Etiology, Concept and Prophy-
laxis of Childbed Fever* (Madison: University of Wisconsin Press, 1983).

14. Markel, "In 1850, Ignaz Semmelweis Saved Lives."

15. Marc Barton, "Ignaz Semmelweis—'The Saviour of Mothers,'"
Past Medical History, March 28, 2016, https://www.pastmedicalhistory
.co.uk/ignaz-semmelweis-the-saviour-of-mothers.

16. "Dr. Semmelweis' Biography," Semmelweis Society International,
http://semmelweis.org/about/dr-semmelweis-biography. See also Tijana
Radeska, "The Sad Destiny of Ignaz Semmelweis—'The Savior of Mothers,'" *The Vintage News*, December 4, 2016, https://www.thevintage
news.com/2016/12/04/the-sad-destiny-of-ignaz-semmelweis-the-savior
-of-mothers. István Benedek, *Ignaz Phillip Semmelweis 1818–1865* (Vienna: H. Bohlau, 1983), 293.

17. W. I. B. Beveridge, *The Art of Scientific Investigation* (New York:
Norton, 1957), 114.

18. Jessie Wright-Mendoza, "The Man Who Invented Modern Infection Control," *JSTOR Daily*, July 21, 2018, https://daily.jstor.org/the-man
-who-invented-modern-infection-control.

19. Tim Bradshaw, "Apple Looks to Face Down Watch Critics," *Financial Times*, May 3, 2017, https://www.ft.com/content/b14d479c-2fbe
-11e7-9555-23ef563ecf9a.

20. Jerome and Powell, *The Disposable Visionary*, 3.

21. Jerome and Powell, *The Disposable Visionary*, 5.

22. Rachel Hodin, "14 Rejection Letters to Famous Artists," *Thought
Catalog*, September 5, 2013, https://thoughtcatalog.com/rachel-hodin
/2013/09/14-rejection-letters-to-famous-artists.

23. Arthur T. Vanderbilt, *The Making of a Bestseller* (Jefferson, NC:
McFarland & Company, 1999), 60.

24. Glenn Leibowitz, "This Simple Writing Strategy Helped John
Grisham Sell Over 300 Million Books," *Inc.*, June 26, 2017, https://www
.inc.com/glenn-leibowitz/this-simple-writing-strategy-helped-john
-grisham-sell-over-300-million-books.html.

25. Sammy McDavid, "A Time to Write," *Mississippi State Alumnus
Magazine*, Winter 1990, http://lib.msstate.edu/grisham/timetowrite.php.

26. Mary Higgins Clark, *Moonlight Becomes You* (New York: Simon & Schuster, 1996), 8.

27. Gordon Tredgold, "31 Quotes to Remind Us of the Importance of Integrity," *Inc.*, January 31, 2017, https://www.inc.com/gordon-tred gold/31-reminders-of-the-importance-of-integrity.html.

28. Jerome and Powell, *The Disposable Visionary*, 84.

29. Bob Sorokanich, "30 Years Ago Today, Chrysler Invented the Mini-van, and Changed History," *Gizmodo*, November 2, 2013, https://gizmodo .com/30-years-ago-today-chrysler-invented-the-minivan-and-1457451986.

30. Joel Siegel, "When Steve Jobs Got Fired by Apple," ABC News, October 6, 2011. See also Paul R. La Monica, "Apple Reaches $1,000,000,000,000 Value," CNN.com, August 2, 2018, https://money.cnn.com/2018/08/02 /investing/apple-one-trillion-market-value/index.html.

Question 9 Is It Too Late?

1. Deborah Headstrom-Page, *From Telegraph to Light Bulb with Thomas Edison* (Nashville: B&H Publishing, 2007), 22.

2. Johnny Davis, "How Lego Clicked: The Super Brand That Reinvented Itself," *Guardian,* June 4, 2017, https://www.theguardian.com /lifeandstyle/2017/jun/04/how-lego-clicked-the-super-brand-that-rein vented-itself.

3. Robertson, *Brick by Brick.* I've also drawn here on John Henley, "The Rebirth of Lego," *Taipei Times*, March 29, 2009, http://www .taipeitimes.com/News/feat/archives/2009/03/29/2003439667 and Richard Feloni, "How Lego Came Back from the Brink of Bankruptcy," *Business Insider*, February 10, 2014, https://www.businessinsider.com/how -lego-made-a-huge-turnaround-2014-2.

4. Steve Denning, "Peggy Noonan on Steve Jobs and Why Big Companies Die," *Forbes*, November 19, 2011, https://www.forbes.com/sites /stevedenning/2011/11/19/peggy-noonan-on-steve-jobs-and-why-big -companies-die.

5. Cited in Keith Sawyer, *Zig Zag* (San Francisco: Jossey-Bass, 2013), 21.

6. Brian Chesky, "Airbnb: The Story No One Believed," YouTube, May 17, 2014, https://www.youtube.com/watch?v=1bAT44QPPHw.

7. Chesky, "Airbnb: The Story No One Believed."

8. Theodore Schleifer, "Airbnb Sold Some Common Stock at a $35 Billion Valuation, but What Is the Company Really Worth?," *Vox*, March 19, 2019, https://www.vox.com/2019/3/19/18272274/airbnb-valuation -common-stock-hoteltonight.

9. Jason Koebler, "10 Years Ago Today, YouTube Launched as a Dating Website," *Vice*, April 23, 2015, https://www.vice.com/en_us/article/78xq jx/10-years-ago-today-youtube-launched-as-a-dating-website.

10. Koebler, "10 Years Ago Today."

11. Stuart Dredge, "YouTube Was Meant to Be a Video-Dating Website," *Guardian*, March 16, 2016, https://www.theguardian.com/technology/2016/mar/16/youtube-past-video-dating-website.

12. Koebler, "10 Years Ago Today."

13. Megan Garber, "Instagram Was First Called 'Burbn,'" *Atlantic*, July 2, 2014, https://www.theatlantic.com/technology/archive/2014/07/instagram-used-to-be-called-brbn/373815.

14. Kurt Carlson, "Using Consumer Problems to Find Blue Oceans," *Forbes*, January 6, 2016, https://www.forbes.com/sites/kurtcarlson/2016/01/06/using-consumer-problems-to-find-blue-ocean.

15. Don Reisinger, "Instagram Is 100 Times More Valuable Than It Was When Facebook Bought It," *Fortune*, June 26, 2018, https://irving.fortune.com/2018/06/26/instagram-facebook-valuation.

16. Sheila Farr, "Starbucks: The Early Years," *HistoryLink*, February 15, 2017, https://historylink.org/File/20292.

17. Sawyer, *Zig Zag*, 20.

18. Sawyer, *Zig Zag*, 21.

19. Starbucks Corp., "Annual Financials for Starbucks Corp.," Market Watch.com, retrieved May 22, 2019, https://www.marketwatch.com/investing/stock/sbux/financials.

20. Watts, *Everything Is Obvious*, 177.

21. Brad Kelechava, "VHS vs Betamax: Standard Format War," *American National Standards Institute*, May 5, 2016, https://blog.ansi.org/2016/05/vhs-vs-betamax-standard-format-war.

22. Watts, *Everything Is Obvious*, 178.

23. Priya Ganapati, "June 4, 1977: VHS Comes To America," *Wired*, June 4, 2010, https://www.wired.com/2010/06/0604vhs-ces.

24. Jennifer Saba and Yinka Adegoke, "Time Warner's Bewkes Skeptical of Netflix Plan," *Reuters*, December 1, 2010, https://www.reuters.com/article/us-media-summit-timewarner/time-warners-bewkes-skeptical-of-netflix-plan-idUSTRE6B10A520101202.

25. Greg Sandovel, "Blockbuster Laughed at Netflix Partnership Offer," CNET.com, December 9, 2010, https://www.cnet.com/news/blockbuster-laughed-at-netflix-partnership-offer.

26. Steve Fuller, "Netflix—Statistics & Facts," Statista.com, retrieved May 14, 2019, https://www.statista.com/topics/842/netflix.

27. "Highest Rated TV Networks among Consumers in the United States as of April 2018," Statista.com, retrieved May 14, 2019, https://www.statista.com/statistics/860060/favorite-tv-network.

28. Bijan Stephen, "Netflix Finally Tied with HBO for Total Wins at the 2018 Emmys," *Verge*, September 18, 2018, https://www.theverge.com/2018/9/18/17873636/netflix-hbo-primetime-networks-breakdown-tie-emmys-2018.

29. "Netflix Revenue 2006–2019," *Macrotrends*, retrieved May 14, 2019, https://www.macrotrends.net/stocks/charts/NFLX/netflix/revenue.

30. Gillian Flaccus, "Oregon Blockbuster Outlasts Others to Become Last on Earth," Associated Press, March 18, 2019, https://www.apnews.com/e543db5476c749038435279edf2fd60f.

31. Connie Guglielmo, "A Steve Jobs Moment That Mattered: Macworld, August 1997," *Forbes*, October 7, 2012, https://www.forbes.com/sites/connieguglielmo/2012/10/07/a-steve-jobs-moment-that-mattered-macworld-august-1997.

32. Nick Whigham, "The Forgotten Microsoft Deal That Saved Apple from Bankruptcy," *New Zealand Herald*, August 5, 2018, https://www.nzherald.co.nz/business/news/article.cfm?c_id=3&objectid=12101418.

33. Justin Bariso, "It Only Took Steve Jobs 5 Words to Give the Best Career Advice You'll Hear Today," *Inc.*, November 27, 2017, https://www.inc.com/justin-bariso/20-years-ago-steve-jobs-revealed-single-word-that-led-to-apples-great-success.html.

34. Zameena Mejia, "Steve Jobs: Here's What Most People Get Wrong about Focus," CNBC.com, October 2, 2018, https://www.cnbc.com/2018/10/02/steve-jobs-heres-what-most-people-get-wrong-about-focus.html.

35. Walter Isaacson, "The Real Leadership Lessons of Steve Jobs," *Harvard Business Review*, April 2012, https://hbr.org/2012/04/the-real-leadership-lessons-of-steve-jobs.

36. Guglielmo, "A Steve Jobs Moment That Mattered."

37. Paul R. La Monica, "Apple Reaches $1,000,000,000,000 Value," CNN.com, August 2, 2018, https://money.cnn.com/2018/08/02/investing/apple-one-trillion-market-value/index.html.

38. Jeff Bezos, "Amazon 2017 Annual Report," https://ir.aboutamazon.com/static-files/917130c5-e6bf-4790-a7bc-cc43ac7fb30a.

39. Jeff Bezos, "2016 Letter to Shareholders," https://ir.aboutamazon.com/static-files/e01cc6e7-73df-4860-bd3d-95d366f29e57.

40. Bezos, "2016 Letter to Shareholders." For a deep dive into what makes Amazon such a dynamic company under Bezos's leadership, see Steve Anderson's book, *The Bezos Letters* (New York: Morgan James, 2019).

41. Kurt Badenhausen, "The World's Most Valuable Brands 2018," *Forbes*, May 23, 2018, https://www.forbes.com/sites/kurtbadenhausen/2018/05/23/the-worlds-most-valuable-brands-2018.

42. Philip Elmer-Dewitt, "Microsoft in the Steve Ballmer Era," *Fortune*, May 27, 2010, https://fortune.com/2010/05/27/microsoft-in-the-steve-ballmer-era.

43. Kurt Eichenwald, "Microsoft's Lost Decade," *Vanity Fair*, July 24, 2012, https://www.vanityfair.com/news/business/2012/08/microsoft-lost-mojo-steve-ballmer.

44. Tom Warren, "Steve Ballmer's 13 Years as Microsoft CEO Leaves a Mixed Legacy with Little Vision," *Verge*, August 26, 2013.

45. Eichenwald, "Microsoft's Lost Decade."

46. David Seidman, "What Were Some of the Key Mistakes Microsoft Made under the Leadership of Steve Ballmer?," *Quora*, February 4, 2018, https://www.quora.com/What-were-some-of-the-key-mistakes-Micro soft-made-under-the-leadership-of-Steve-Ballmer.

47. David Lieberman, "CEO Forum: Microsoft's Ballmer Having a 'Great Time,'" *USA Today*, April 29, 2007, https://usatoday30.usatoday .com/money/companies/management/2007-04-29-ballmer-ceo-forum -usat_N.htm.

48. Eichenwald, "Microsoft's Lost Decade."

49. Satya Nadella and Greg Shaw, *Hit Refresh* (New York: Harper-Collins, 2017), 66–67.

50. Harry McCracken, "Satya Nadella's Microsoft Vision Is Strikingly Different from Steve Ballmer's Microsoft Vision," *Technologizer*, July 10, 2014, https://www.technologizer.com/2014/07/10/satya-nadella -microsoft.

51. Jordan Novet, "How Microsoft Bounced Back," CNBC, December 3, 2018, https://www.cnbc.com/2018/12/03/microsoft-recovery-how -satya-nadella-did-it.html.

52. Rachel Layne, "Microsoft Reaches $1 Trillion Market Value for the First Time," *CBS News*, April 25, 2019, https://www.cbsnews.com /news/microsoft-1-trillion-market-value-reached-today.

53. Helen Edwards and Dave Edwards, "One Out of Every 10 American Companies Is a 'Zombie,'" *Quartz*, December 5, 2017, https://qz.com/11 41732/one-in-every-10-american-companies-is-a-zombie.

54. Sara Estes, "The Persistence of Vinyl," The Bitter Southerner, retrieved March 18, 2019, https://bittersoutherner.com/united-record -pressing#.XS4KkHspBPY.

55. Bill Rosenblatt, "Vinyl Is Bigger Than We Thought. Much Bigger," *Forbes*, September 18, 2018, https://www.forbes.com/sites/billrosenblatt /2018/09/18/vinyl-is-bigger-than-we-thought-much-bigger.

56. Estes, "The Persistence of Vinyl."

57. Ryan Lambie, "How Marvel Went from Bankruptcy to Billions," *Den of Geek!* April 17, 2018, https://www.denofgeek.com/us/books -comics/marvel/243710/how-marvel-went-from-bankruptcy-to-billions.

58. Lambie, "How Marvel Went from Bankruptcy to Billions."

59. Ben Fritz, *The Big Picture* (Boston: Houghton, 2018), 63.

60. Box Office Mojo, retrieved March 23, 2019, https://www.boxoffice mojo.com/franchises/chart/?id=ironmanfranchise.htm. See also Amy Kaufman, "'Iron Man 3' Makes $1 Billion Worldwide, $300 Million Domestically," *Los Angeles Times*, May 17, 2013, https://www.latimes.com

/entertainment/envelope/cotown/la-et-ct-box-office-iron-man-3-makes
-billion-dollars-20130517-story.html.

61. David Goldman, "Disney to Buy Marvel for $4 Billion," CNN.com,
August 31, 2009, https://money.cnn.com/2009/08/31/news/companies
/disney_marvel.

62. Scott Mendelson, "Box Office: 'Black Panther' Sinks 'Titanic,'
Tops $1.3 Billion, Wins 'Black Jeopardy,'" *Forbes*, April 9, 2018, https://
www.forbes.com/sites/scottmendelson/2018/04/09/box-office-black-pan
ther-sinks-titanic-passes-1-3-billion-wins-black-jeopardy.

63. Jonathan Berr, "'Black Panther' Merchandise Is Also Striking
Gold," *CBS News*, March 6, 2018, https://www.cbsnews.com/news
/black-panther-merchandise-is-also-striking-gold.

64. "The Biggest Business Comebacks of the Past 20 Years," *Fast
Company*, March 17, 2015, https://www.fastcompany.com/3042431
/the-biggest-business-comebacks-of-the-past-20-years.

65. "'Avengers: Endgame' Leaves Box Office Records in the Dust,"
FoxNews.com, April 28, 2019, https://www.foxnews.com/entertainment
/avengers-endgame-box-office-record.

66. Craig Smith, "20 Interesting Flickr Stats and Facts (2019)," Expand
edramblings.com, https://expandedramblings.com/index.php/flickr-stats/.

67. Jonathan Dame, "Number of Daily Slack Users Surpasses 10 Million," Search Unified Communications, https://searchunifiedcommunica
tions.techtarget.com/news/252456752/Number-of-daily-Slack-users-sur
passes-10-million.

68. Tomio Geron, "A Look Back at Yahoo's Flickr Acquisition for
Lessons Today," Techcrunch.com, August 23, 2014, https://techcrunch
.com/2014/08/23/flickrs-acquisition-9-years-later/.

69. "A Sad Announcement from Tiny Speck," GlitchtheGame.com,
retrieved May 14, 2019, https://www.glitchthegame.com/closing/.

70. Knowlton Thomas, "Seven Interesting Facts You Probably Didn't
Know about Canadian Entrepreneur Stewart Butterfield," Techvibes.com,
January 1, 2015, https://techvibes.com/2015/01/07/facts-stewart-butter
field-slack-2015-01-07.

71. In fact, the name stands for "Searchable Log of All Conversation
and Knowledge." Megan Hernbroth, "Slack, the Newly-Public Chat App
Worth about $20 Billion, Has a Hidden Meaning behind Its Name,"
Business Insider, June 20, 2019, https://www.businessinsider.com/where
-did-slack-get-its-name-2016-9.

72. Alex Hern, "Why Slack Is Worth $1Bn: It's Trying to Change
How We Work," *Guardian*, November 3, 2014, https://www.theguardian
.com/technology/2014/nov/03/why-slack-is-worth-1bn-work-chat-app.
See also Knowlton Thomas, "Slack Is the World's Fastest Startup to Reach
$2 Billion Ever," Techvibes.com, April 26, 2015, https://techvibes.com

/2015/04/25/slack-the-worlds-fastest-startup-to-reach-2-billion-in-hist
ory-2015-04-24.

73. Holden Page, "Slack's Startup Investments as It Preps for Direct
Listing," CrunchbaseNews.com, May 14, 2019, https://news.crunchbase
.com/news/slacks-startup-investments-as-it-preps-for-direct-listing/.

Question 10 Are You Ready?

1. George Bernard Shaw, *Back to Methuselah*, Part 1, Act 1.
2. Derek Thompson, "The Mysterious Death of Entrepreneurship in
America," *Atlantic*, May 12, 2014, https://www.theatlantic.com/business
/archive/2014/05/entrepreneurship-in-america-is-dying-wait-what-does
-that-actually-mean/362097. Edward C. Prescott and Lee E. Ohanian, "Behind the Productivity Plunge: Fewer Startups," *Wall Street Journal*, June
25, 2014, https://www.wsj.com/articles/behind-the-productivity-plunge
-fewer-startups-1403737197. Stephen Harrison, "Start-Ups Aren't Cool
Anymore," *Atlantic*, December 5, 2018, https://www.theatlantic.com
/business/archive/2018/12/milennial-start-up/567793. Leigh Buchanan,
"American Entrepreneurship Is Actually Vanishing. Here's Why," Inc
.com, May 2015, https://www.inc.com/magazine/201505/leigh-buchanan
/the-vanishing-startups-in-decline.html. Noah Smith, "America's Startup
Scene Is Looking Anemic," Bloomberg.com, June 7, 2018, https://www
.bloomberg.com/opinion/articles/2018-06-07/america-s-startup
-scene-is-looking-anemic. Dan Kopf, "The US Startup Is Disappearing,"
Quartz, June 20, 2018, https://qz.com/1309824/the-us-startup-company-is
-disappearing-and-thats-bad-for-the-economy. "Dynamism in Retreat,"
Economic Innovation Group, February 2017, https://eig.org/dynamism.
3. Buchanan, "American Entrepreneurship Is Actually Vanishing."
4. Erika Andersen, "It Seemed Like a Good Idea at the Time: 7 of the
Worst Business Decisions Ever Made," *Forbes*, October 4, 2013, https://
www.forbes.com/sites/erikaandersen/2013/10/04/it-seemed-like-a-good
-idea-at-the-time-7-of-the-worst-business-decisions-ever-made.
5. Bloomberg, "Netflix Looks Like a Loser. But Here's Why It's Probably a Winner," *Fortune*, August 8, 2017, https://fortune.com/2017/08/15
/netflix-looks-like-loser-feels-like-winner.
6. Melanie Warner, "Can Amazon Be Saved? Jeff Bezos Writes a New
Script. Too Bad for Investors It Is More Fiction Than Fact," *CNN Money*,
November 26, 2001, https://money.cnn.com/magazines/fortune/fortune
_archive/2001/11/26/314112/index.htm.
7. Arthur C. Clarke, *Profiles of the Future* (New York: Harper, 1962), 1.
8. Neil D. Shortland, Laurence J. Alison, and Joseph M. Moran,
Conflict: How Soldiers Make Impossible Decisions (New York: Oxford
University Press, 2019), 27.

Thanks

Everyone likes to think their work is original. But as Solomon observed almost three thousand years ago, "there's nothing new under the sun." All work—especially writing—is derivative. I have done my best to cite my sources and give credit where credit is due. But beyond direct citations, I have been influenced by a plethora of people who have shaped my thinking over the years.

I have had the privilege of working with numerous business coaches over the years, including Daniel Harkavy, Dan Meub, Ilene Muething, and Dan Sullivan. They have helped me write vision statements for my own companies or said things that ultimately found their way into those statements. It would be hard to overestimate their impact on my life. They are the major reason for my success.

My thinking about vision has also been influenced by numerous authors, including Jon Acuff, Jack Canfield, Jim Collins, Stephen R. Covey, Ian Morgan Cron, Joe Dispenza, Ray Edwards, Jason Fried, Dean Graziosi, Verne Harnish, Napoleon Hill, Lewis Howes, Patrick Lencioni, Bruce H.

Lipton, John C. Maxwell, Stu McLaren, Bryan and Shannon Miles, Dan Miller, Donald Miller, Cal Newport, Amy Porterfield, Skip Prichard, Dave Ramsey, Tony Robbins, Andy Stanley, Tim Tassopoulos, and Jeff Walker. Though not all of these have written about vision, they all inspire me with the clarity of their vision for a better, more compelling future.

This book would have never happened without the collaboration of my writing and research team. Bob DeMoss interviewed me, studied the various frameworks I shared in my blog posts, podcasts, and workshops, and then wrote the first draft of the manuscript. Joel Miller, our chief content officer at Michael Hyatt & Co., then shaped, sculpted, and redrafted the manuscript. They both worked tirelessly to get this book into its current form. I am grateful for their servant-hearted teamwork. Larry Wilson, one of our senior content creators, also helped with the research.

I am also grateful for my publishing team at Baker Books, including Dwight Baker, Brian Vos, Mark Rice, Patti Brinks, and Barb Barnes. This is our fourth book project, and I couldn't be happier with our partnership. They are the consummate professionals, providing helpful feedback and support every step of the way. They provide the reach and distribution of a large publisher and the intimacy and care of a small one. I am grateful for their belief in me.

My literary agent, Bryan Norman of Alive Literary Agency, is also an important part of our publishing team. Over our years together he has become a trusted advisor, advocating for me with Baker and for Baker with me. He is the perfect liaison, always insistent on win-win relationships.

My wife, Gail, is more than my spouse. She is my best friend, intimate ally, and biggest cheerleader. She also constantly challenges me to speak and write in a way that is clearer, simpler, and more engaging. She takes it upon herself to advocate for the reader and does it brilliantly.

I especially want to thank our BusinessAccelerator® clients. As I have talked about vision over the years in our coaching workshops, they were the ones who initially requested— no, demanded!—that I write about this topic and put my thoughts into a book. Nothing I do professionally is more rewarding than spending time with them. To witness their growth and transformation is why I do what I do.

Last, but certainly not least, I want to express my deepest appreciation to my team at Michael Hyatt & Co. They are truly the best team I have ever had. They constantly motivate me to be my best. Working with them is a joy. These include Courtney Baker, Suzie Barbour, Verbs Boyer, Mike Burns, Ora Corr, Susan Caldwell, Chad Cannon, Aleshia Curry, Trey Dunavant, Andrew Fockel, Natalie Fockel, Megan Greer, Jamie Hess, Adam Hill, Marissa Hyatt, Jim Kelly, Sarah McElroy, John Meese, Joel Miller, Megan Hyatt Miller, Renee Murphy, Charae Price, Mandi Rivieccio, Tessa Robert, Danielle Rodgers, Deidra Romero, Neal Samudre, Shana Smith, Jarrod Souza, Blake Stratton, Emi Tanke, Becca Turner, Elizabeth White, Larry Wilson, Kyle Wyley, and Dave Yankowiak.

Index

Michael Hyatt is the founder and CEO of Michael Hyatt & Co., which helps leaders get the focus they need to win at work *and* succeed at life. Formerly chairman and CEO of Thomas Nelson Publishers, Michael is also the creator of the *Full Focus Planner* and a *New York Times*, *Wall Street Journal*, and *USA Today* bestselling author of several books, including *Free to Focus*, *Your Best Year Ever*, *Living Forward*, and *Platform*. His work has been featured by the *Wall Street Journal*, *Forbes*, *Inc.*, *Fast Company*, *Businessweek*, *Entrepreneur*, and other publications. Michael has been married to his wife, Gail, for more than forty years. They have five daughters, three sons-in-law, and nine grandchildren. They live just outside Nashville, Tennessee. Learn more at MichaelHyatt.com.

Slay Distractions, Reduce Your Task List,
AND FREE YOURSELF FROM INTERRUPTIONS

Reinvent your productivity with a total productivity system proven to help you reclaim hours of your workweek while achieving more.

CLOSE THE GAP BETWEEN REALITY
AND YOUR DREAMS

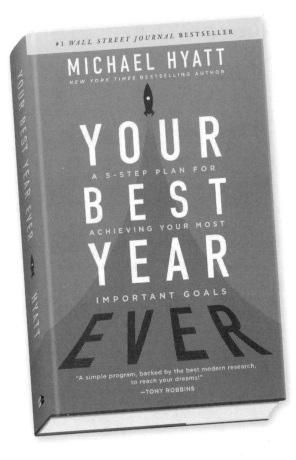

Discover a powerful, proven, research-backed process for setting and achieving life-changing goals.

In the first year of the program, the average client experiences . . .

 67% Growth in revenue

 11 Reclaimed hours per week

 64% Increase in confidence

 66% More vacation time

*These results are self-reported and unverified. Your results will vary depending on numerous factors, including your implementation of the program's principles and strategies.

Find out more at
businessaccelerator.com/vision

Draft Your Vision in Just Minutes

Introducing . . .

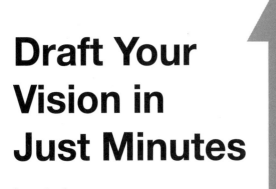

Create a clear and compelling Vision Script with Michael Hyatt & Company's free tool, **the Vision Scripter.**

The Vision Scripter offers:

Video coaching from Michael Hyatt on how to create a compelling vision.

An interactive web-based portal to draft your vision and share it with your team.

Questions and cues to make writing your vision simple and easy.

Go to
VisionDrivenLeader.com/visionscripter
to get started today.

Connect with

BakerBooks

Relevant. Intelligent. Engaging.

Sign up for announcements about new and upcoming titles at

BakerBooks.com/SignUp

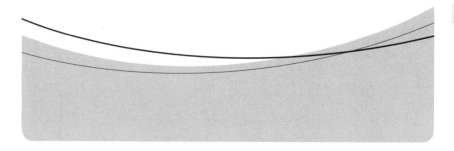

@ReadBakerBooks